From the Publisher of *FineScale Modeler*

BUILDING AND PAINTING

MODEL DINOSAURS

RAY RIMELL

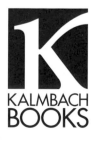

KALMBACH
BOOKS

I would like to dedicate this book to the memory of my Grandmother Kate Rimell (1895–1993).

Printed in the United States of America

98 99 00 01 02 03 04 05 06   9 8 7 6 5 4 3 2 1

For more information, visit our website at
    http://www.kalmbach.com

Publisher's Cataloging in Publication
(Provided by Quality Books, Inc.)

Rimell, Ray.
    Building and painting model dinosaurs / by Ray Rimell.
  — 1st ed.
    p. cm.
    Includes bibliographical references.
    ISBN: 0-89024-270-4

    1. Dinosaurs—Models. 2. Models and modelmaking. I. Title.

QE862.D5R56 1997   567.9'022
                                  QBI97-41266

Book and cover design: Kristi Ludwig

(All models and photos by the author)

CONTENTS

ACKNOWLEDGMENTS

I would like to take this opportunity to thank the following individuals who have helped me tremendously as I worked on this book and various other dinosaur model projects: Dave Alden (Saurian Studios); Janice Batchelor (Natural History Museum); John Burns (Kit Collectors' Clearing House); John Carlson and Jane Sullivan (Monstrosities); Dave Chenault (Vector Models); John Cundell (Claserprint); Gary Dovell (The Dupe Connection); Mike Evans; Mike Fredericks (*The Prehistoric Times*); Graham Hales (AA Hales Ltd.); Steve Harvey (Wiccart); T. Hirayama (Tamiya International Division); Yoshi Hoashi (Horizon Hobbies); Tony James (Comet Miniatures); Shelley Jones Fenleigh (Invicta Plastics Ltd.); John Kuehnert; Dan LoRusso (The Dinosaur Studio); Nick Lytton (Tyrannus Imports); Bob Morales (Dragon Attack!); Motohiro Suzuki (Tamiya International Division); W. G. Hazlewood (Wiltshire Timbercrafts); various members of The Dinosaur Society (U.S. and U.K.); and Terry Spohn, Bob Hayden, and Paul Boyer of Kalmbach Publishing Co. I'd also like to thank Mrs. Julie Stilwell for typing the manuscript. Last, but by no means least, warmest appreciation to my partner Angela Hogan for continual helpful advice and assistance and for her forbearance when dozens of large, scaly creatures began gradually to invade the household. Without her encouragement this book could not have been written. *RLR*

INTRODUCTION

With the worldwide success of the movie *Jurassic Park* in 1993 and its sequel *Lost World,* interest in dinosaurs has never been higher. For the hobbyist, similarly, never have there been so many good-quality dinosaur model kits available. An ever-growing number of companies in both the United States and Japan continue to release a large selection of such models in the wake of Steven Spielberg's original blockbuster, but not all of them are mere *JP* spin-offs. Many had been planned well before the movie's release. Most are based on the very latest scientific research and thus offer quantum-leap improvements over earlier dinosaur kits. Now after the *JP* sequel and with other dinosaur movies already in production, more models are being unleashed onto the world market.

Yet even before recent movies dazzled us with their computer-generated images, interest in exotic and spellbinding prehistoric animals was always high. Witness the heavy attendance of natural history museum dinosaur galleries and the many dinomation exhibitions worldwide. There are countless thousands of dinosaur enthusiasts on every continent: book and stamp collectors, amateur fossil hunters, research students, artists and sculptors, quite apart from the professional scientists and paleontologists to whom we owe such a great debt for continually expanding our knowledge of these wonderful, long-extinct creatures. Relatively few of these "dinophiles" are keen, experienced modelers, though doubtless most would welcome a miniature *Mamenchisaurus* on the mantelpiece, wish for shelves stacked with stegosaurs, or cherish a *Chasmosaurus* in their bedside cabinet.

But suppose they don't feel they have the necessary spare time to build "difficult" dinosaur models or lack the confidence even to try? Perhaps the purchase of those exacting display sculptures from professional, skilled artisans lies beyond their financial means. What then?

With some notable exceptions, most of the commercially available, ready-made dinosaur models frequently found in shopping malls are anatomically incorrect or out of date. The current crop of model kits is far superior. But how to turn these boxes of bits into the kind of quality miniatures that can be seen displayed in the very best of natural history museum collections?

I hope that this book will go some way to answering these questions, guiding and inspiring those who have never even built model kits before. Encouragingly, dinosaurs are among the easiest types of model to make. Within the following pages, you will learn how to get the best from plastic, vinyl, and resin kits before moving on to making basic improvements, trying simple and then more involved conversions, and mastering all-important painting techniques. You will also learn to build dioramas involving several models in special set pieces.

With the aid of selected examples from all the major known dinosaurian groups, I have striven to provide the impetus for dinosaur enthusiasts of all persuasions to try their hand at modeling these marvelous beasts. Don't worry about having to match contest-winning experts or becoming a fully qualified paleontologist to enjoy this absorbing hobby. I wouldn't place myself in either category—I'm not a dinosaur expert! But the plain truth is that dinosaurs are great fun and so are building and painting models of them. If this joy shines through the following chapters, then I've more than accomplished the purpose of this book.

Ray Rimell, 1998

TAKING IT EASY

That old cliché about learning to walk before trying to run may be well-worn, but it's particularly appropriate for most hobby activities. Modeling is no exception. So before embarking on dinosaur kit building (described more fully in the following chapter), newcomers to the hobby may want to practice some easy techniques first. For such purposes I advocate any of the less expensive, ready-molded, one-piece dinosaur models, the best examples of which are usually to be found in souvenir shops of most natural history museums. Although some of these models do vary in quality, the majority of them can be recommended. Readily available and, more important, generally inexpensive, they provide the basis for gaining plenty

of useful experience without the risk of making more costly mistakes later on attempting kit building for the first time.

Museum-authenticated models are of course just the tip of the proverbial iceberg. Hundreds of other plastic or rubber dinosaur models are available in toy stores or gas stations, as special offers with cereals and cookies, or in malls and supermarkets, although most of them are junk as far as modelers are concerned. Cheaply produced and often crudely detailed, these brightly colored caricatures are designed naturally enough to appeal to kids who are not supposed to notice, or to care, that their brand new *T. Rex* looks like Godzilla, or that the floppy, rubber *Pteranodon* their mom just bought

looks like a vampire bat. The cheapskates who produce such rubbish should take time out for a little market research. Most five-year-olds could point out all the mistakes while reeling off the dinosaurs' correct scientific names with ease—and spelling them correctly, too! Many kids are well-versed in such matters, to the frequent surprise of parents and teachers alike.

When I was at kindergarten in the late 1950s, I had an all-consuming passion for dinosaurs, collecting and reading everything available on the subject. Despite my teachers' efforts to rechannel my enthusiasm toward other topics, I continued to draw dinosaurs and write about them for a long time until other interests supplanted them. Reading Michael Crichton's *Jurassic Park* many years later rekindled a long-dormant fascination. All this serves merely as a cautionary tale. If your kids display a keen interest in a subject, encourage them all you can; and if it's dinosaurs, don't buy them any of those cheap and nasty toy dinos. Shop around and be more selective. You'll soon be told which are the best ones to buy—I guarantee it!

So let's select some models and begin honing our skills. I would recommend three product lines of dinosaur replicas for their scientific accuracy, constant scale, and sheer diversity of dinosaur groups they embrace. Most well known is The Carnegie Collection, a continually expanding product line manufactured in China for Safari Ltd. All the dinosaurs and prehistoric reptiles in the series are sculpted under the guidance of the Carnegie Museum of Natural History in Pittsburgh to a constant scale of 1/40. All are pre-painted, and recent releases incorporate the latest thinking in dinosaur appearance and habits. Sets and display items are also available.

Another series is that produced by Invicta Plastics of the United Kingdom in association with London's Natural History Museum. It is available in unpainted or painted form to a constant scale of 1/45. There are currently 22 models available, the product line including other prehistoric animals, such as a woolly mammoth, *Pteranodon, Dimetrodon,* and marine reptiles as well as a modern mammal, a blue whale. Invicta also produces various grouped sets of models plus plaster-casting and painting kits that include selected models.

Most recent, and highly praised by many paleontologists, is the 1/40 Battat product line, the masters of which are sculpted by Greg Wenzel and Don LoRusso for Boston's Museum of Science. Eighteen models are currently available, and many subjects are unique to Battat. These new models reflect the very latest fossil evidence and theories, while their colorful paint schemes are very attractive.

All these series are well suited for our purpose. By using them we can acquire some of the techniques that can later be applied to larger and more specialized dinosaur kits that are currently available. Also, by virtue of their comparatively small scales (I mean size, not skin!), these inexpensive museum models will prove invaluable for background diorama props, as will be outlined more fully in chapter 5. But here we go, running before we can walk. There are some important things to tell you before we start on our very first dinosaur model.

BEFORE YOU BEGIN

Once you have decided to pursue modeling as a hobby, you will need to obtain a number of tools to help you. First, knives. My preference is for surgeon's scalpels. They are light and easy to handle, and there is a fairly wide selection of blades. These are sharper than most hobby knives, and the blades will last longer if used carefully. You could also try X-acto hobby knives or similar; these are very good, although not quite as sharp as scalpels.

Adhesives come next. Both tube and liquid polystyrene cements are available for plastic kit building. The latter is best, but mixing the two together is often useful. White glue (PVA) as used by woodworkers is a versatile adhesive, also ideal for diorama work and fine-joint filling—as we shall see.

For vinyl and resin kits, two-pack epoxy glues (the quick-set

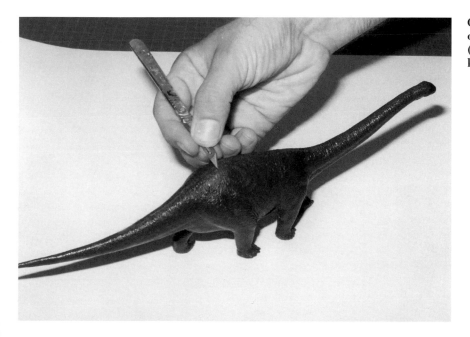

Carefully remove the centerline seam of Invicta's 1/45 scale *Cetiosaurus* (whale lizard) with a sharp hobby knife. Keep the blade sharp.

variety) are recommended, but best of all are the cyanoacrylate (CA) super glues. Zap and Loctite are good brands to go for; aim for medium-size bottles from the hobby store unless you do a lot of modeling. Larger sizes can be wasteful because the glue thickens up over time, while the small tubes are poor value for the money.

You'll also need a good set of files, and various grades of wet or dry carbide paper available from auto stores. Also useful are the Flexi-File and a sanding block or you can make your own by gluing a section of carbide paper to a flat piece of wood. Get hold of a cutting mat, too. For cutting purposes, small wire cutters or tin snips are handy, while artists' masking tape and rubber bands prove invaluable for holding assembled parts together while the glue dries. My modeling toolbox also includes wooden and plastic toothpicks, two or three fine-tipped tweezers for handling small parts, razor saws for use on resins, a pin vise, and a selection of small drill bits. Later you may wish to purchase more-expensive aids, such as a stand magnifier, a small cordless drill, a motor tool for use with sanding bits, and an airbrush with compressor for painting. We'll look more

closely at paints and brushes in chapter 4.

To keep all this in tidy order, those tough plastic toolboxes available in auto stores are ideal. You can keep all your tools in various compartments and organize them to suit yourself. When you've finished for the day, just pack it all away. When you start again, everything is presorted and easy to find—or should be!

Ample work space is paramount. Few of us have large customized workshops, but at the very least you'll need a sturdy table, a good light, and adequate ventilation. For safety's sake, invest in a pair of safety goggles; these are essential when using scalpels to cut and trim plastic, resin, and vinyl parts. Even modelers with years of experience break knife blades, and I have the scars to prove it. For hand mixing two-pack fillers and adhesives, I recommend disposable rubber gloves, especially if you have sensitive skin. This may sound like paranoia, but you can't be too careful. Better safe than sorry.

GETTING STARTED

Okay, so we've cleared a space on the dining room table and obtained some tools. Now we're ready to go. As our introduction to

the hobby, I've selected Invicta's *Cetiosaurus,* a typical example of a good, one-piece, ready-made museum model, but almost any other one will do. It's your choice. *Cetiosaurus* (whale lizard) was a sauropod, an enormous dinosaur whose bulky body and long neck and tail are many people's conception of a typical dinosaur. They make great modeling subjects, too. Invicta's 1/45 scale *Cetiosaurus* is molded in a soft polypropylene quite unlike the hard polystyrene used for plastic kits. The Invicta *Cetiosaurus* (model no. 3256) measures 13⅜″ nose to tail and, apart from the lurid purple color it's molded in, is an authentic representation of the Jurassic sauropod. The painted version of the same model is much more realistic, but the highly glossy finish may not appeal to many serious modelers.

Because of the molding process, these types of models normally bear seams of "flash" (or "flashing," excess plastic creeping from the mold halves under pressure). Most obvious is that which runs along the model's centerline; others will occur around the legs. These really should be removed before painting or, at least, rendered less visible. To remove this unwanted material, exercise ex-

The copyright declaration and model details are usually located under the model, where they are often invisible. Remove the raised ones, if you want, by shaving; fill those that are engraved.

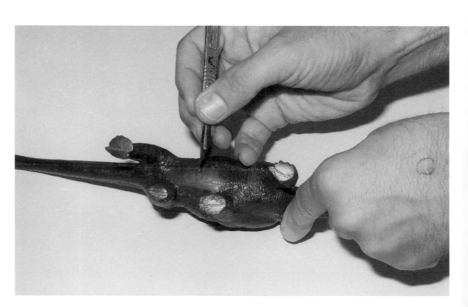

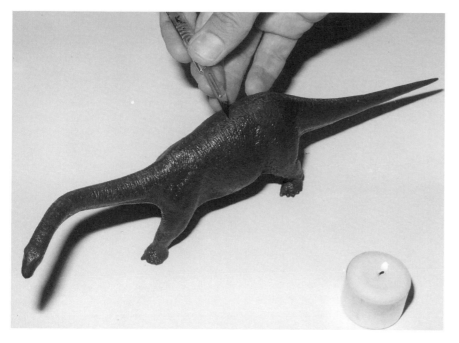

The Invicta models may be modified by using a mild heat source (a candle or night-light) to bend necks and tails. Hold the model near the flame—but not in it!—and bend to the desired shape. Be extremely careful; do not stand lit candles anywhere near adhesives, paints, or spray canisters.

treme care because the kind of soft plastic used can be awkward to work with. It cannot be sanded; the flash merely becomes ragged and obstinately stays put. The only sure way I've found is to carefully shave it off using a sharp scalpel or hobby knife, an operation that demands not only great care but also patience and a steady hand. Safety tip: always cut away from you to avoid accidents. These knife blades are extremely sharp!

Manufacturers such as Battat, Carnegie, and Invicta understandably incorporate the model name with their own copyright impression under the tails or bellies of their replicas. If you consider these obtrusive or inappropriate for your carefully painted scale model, you can shave them off with the knife or treat them with model filler, such as Squadron's White Putty. When it is dry, carefully scrape the putty using the flat of the knife blade.

PAINTING

The soft property of the plastic makes painting the museum models a task to be carefully approached. Since the plastic is not inert, the very flexibility of the model can

Use acrylic paints (Tamiya's, in this case) to provide a basic overall flesh color to the *Cetiosaurus.* Use a fairly wide brush and remember: two thin coats are always better than one heavy one.

You can use drybrushing or highlighting techniques (see chapter 5) to accentuate the molded detail. Prepare a lighter version of the base color by mixing in white. Brush out on scrap paper (not newspaper, since the ink will come off) or card so that only the barest amount of paint remains on the tips of the bristles. Do this before brushing the model.

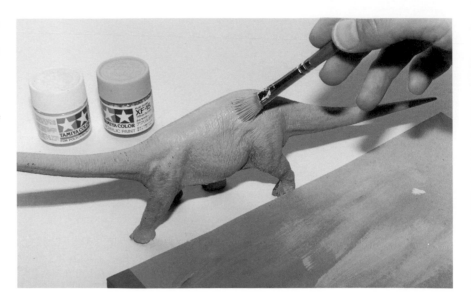

result in paint flaking off, whichever brand or type you use. To help alleviate this problem, first wash the model thoroughly in warm water mixed with a little detergent. Make this a habit for all models before painting. Cleaning removes the original mold grease and the natural oils from your hands. Thereafter the model should be handled as little as possible and then only with a lint-free cloth; or you can use cotton or disposable rubber gloves. In any event, keep models free from grease before painting. No paint takes well to uncleaned surfaces, and an initial primer coat of a light color is recommended.

Acrylic paints (such as those produced by MRC/Tamiya) give the best results for polypropylene models. Unlike oil-base enamels or water colors, they are less likely to flake off when the model is handled. Incidentally, Invicta's own dinosaur painting kit provides four prehistoric animals in a much softer, more flexible material than that of the standard models. Also included are six primary acrylic colors that are thinned or mixed with water and that provide a perfect finish with no flaking. Well recommended.

Since chapter 4 deals in depth with various painting techniques that may be applied to model dinosaurs, it is not necessary to discuss them here. But since we are at an introductory stage, the following guidelines may prove helpful now. By all means, turn to the painting chapter if basic techniques are familiar to you, but please don't forget to turn back to chapter 3 later on. I'd really hate for you to miss anything!

PRACTICE MAKES PERFECT

For the *Cetiosaurus* I came up with a fairly simple scheme of two contrasting colors, although you could paint it in one overall shade or in three, four, or even five different colors. It's your choice. The model shown

was painted a pale flesh and sand overall, which served as a basic primer color, followed by large upper areas of earth brown. Tamiya's acrylics offer many military camouflage colors that are ideal for dinosaurs, too. We're never going to know what colors the dinosaurs were, since such features are not preserved in the fossil record. Nobody, therefore, can criticize your chosen scheme. Here your guess is as good as that of the most dedicated paleontologist or anyone else's for that matter, and that includes model contest judges. We'll be returning to this topic later, but don't start looking for Federal Standards codes in the appendixes. I didn't come up with any.

Tamiya acrylics provide XF-15 flat flesh and XF-32 flat earth. But if you have only primary colors available, these can be mixed using yellow, red, and white for the flesh; red, black, yellow, and brown for the darker shade. Mix the colors thoroughly in a suitable container (small glass jars or bottles will do) and apply a thin overall coat of flesh to the model using a moderate-size, stiff nylon-bristled brush. Don't be too surprised if a second coat is required—it's easy to miss small areas on scaly, textured surfaces. Do follow the manufacturer's guides on the paint jars. Stir the paint well and leave plenty of time (at least 24 hours) between coats.

For the cetiosaur's upper, darker color, I used a finer brush to first mark the division line, which can be curved, as shown, or straighter if you like. If it helps, use a soft pencil and lightly mark out the area (or areas) you want to fill in.

Once satisfied with the results, you may wish to give the finish an extra dimension. The skin and muscle details of museum models are usually very realistic and well-molded but will look even better if emphasized. We'll be covering shading and highlighting techniques later, but for now our *Cetiosaurus* won't object

In the foreground is the modified and painted *Cetiosaurus*. Beyond it is the standard unpainted Invicta model.

Use a much finer brush to apply the demarcation lines for the second color as shown. Then with a larger brush, fill in the upper areas. Colors and patterns are up to you—it's your model. Free expression is one of the delights of dinosaur modeling.

to an overall coat of matte polyurethane varnish to which a small amount of dark brown enamel paint has been added.

Use a small jar for mixing and continually stir the tinted varnish while painting the model overall. Use a large brush. This technique should result in the model's skin folds and molded detail catching and holding the intermixed paint, while overall varnishing will tone down and darken the base colors for a more somber appearance.

As a final touch, the eyes can be painted gloss black with a fine brush or marker pen. The claws, or toes, can be painted either dark gray or ivory, as desired.

If you wish to alter the chosen color schemes of ready-painted models, you can overpaint them. But avoid using any cellulose-base sprays for initial priming, since these are likely to attack and craze the original paintwork. A cellulose-base paint may, of course, be considered an advantage, acting as a form of paint-stripper. But it will prove a messy and time-consuming enterprise and is not advisable. It may also damage the plastic. Best apply your new scheme with acrylics.

If you are unhappy with your first attempts, providing you used water-base acrylics and don't delay, the colors can be washed off in water and you can then start again. This is possible, of course, only if the model has not been varnished; if it has been, just paint directly over the top of the varnish.

To finish the featured model, I sought a simple base to show it off. Try a small, sawed-off varnished tree branch, available at gardening stores or florists. These wood slices are usually varnished on one side only, and the model's feet can be glued or pinned to them directly using one of the cyanoacrylate super glues (such as Zap) or merely placed on the plinth unsecured. Additional work to the base is optional (turn

Simple two-color schemes

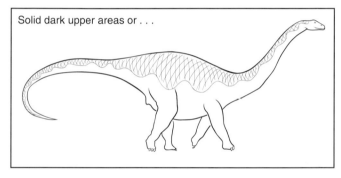

Solid dark upper areas or . . .

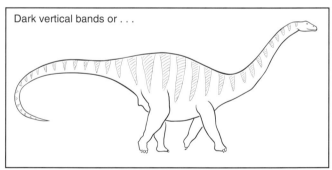

Dark vertical bands or . . .

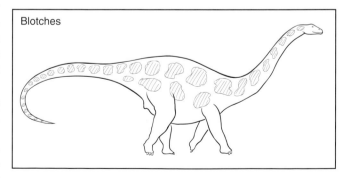

Blotches

Another easy painting effect is stippling. Here an old stiff brush is used to dab light yellow blotches over a basic green finish. When it is dry, use dark brown or black over the top as further mottling. Practice on scrap card or paper first. The model is Invicta's unique 1/20 scale *Troodon*.

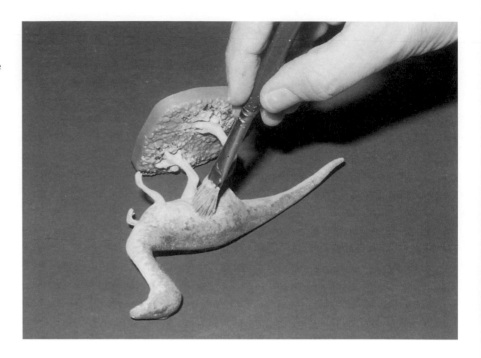

to chapter 5 for ideas on terrain and vegetation effects).

I hope the foregoing will help you develop new-found skills and result in more lifelike replicas. Certainly the models will look more interesting than when first purchased, and you will have stamped a little of your individuality on them. The key word is PRACTICE. Use these relatively inexpensive museum models to improve your painting and display skills because it will be simple enough to make such models appear even more realistic by incorporating them into their own carefully designed dioramas. So don't dismiss them once you've moved up a few notches to more advanced kits. Many museum models make great little replicas in their own right, providing wonderful diorama background material when combined with larger scale models for enforced perspective.

2

STARTING WITH KITS

Ask the average 8- or 80-year-old to name any dinosaur off the top of their heads, and nine times out of ten *Tyrannosaurus Rex* will be mentioned. Even if they have never seen the spectacular recreation of *T. Rex* in *Jurassic Park* and *Lost World,* most people can easily visualize that terrifying, dominant meat eater of the Cretaceous world, until recently the ultimate predator. Not surprisingly, *Tyrannosaurus* has been, and remains still, one of the most modeled dinosaurs, and both toy and kit manufacturers have not been slow to exploit its mass appeal.

PLASTIC KITS

Recent releases have had the benefit of modern research, and the best plastic "tyrant lizard" produced thus far is unquestionably Tamiya's version. It is the second in their 1/35 scale dinosaur series, which appeared in 1993. It makes an ideal choice for your first dinosaur plastic kit.

Tamiya's kit thoughtfully offers a choice of leg parts to enable either a walking or a running pose to be modeled, while the jaw can be open or closed thanks to yet more alternative pieces. The diorama base—a hallmark of this series—includes a separate tree stump, a *Parasaurolophus* skull, and bones, plus two cycad trees. The latter have plastic trunks with green crepe paper leaves, which are cut out and glued to the coated green wire stems supplied, the latter fixed through holes in the tops of the tree trunk. It is all very carefully thought out and executed superbly.

If you are building your first dinosaur, then this tyrannosaur would be ideal, as would any one

of the Tamiya kits. Fairly simple to construct, they come with generally well fitting parts and in decent sizes, thus avoiding difficulties usually associated with very small pieces.

The instruction leaflets Tamiya provides are a model of their kind. They should be carefully read and studied before attempting to begin any work. Never ignore kit instructions! Separate the parts from the runners and frames only as you need them, using your modeling

knife or nail clippers, cutting or snipping as far away from the molded part as the plastic will allow. Afterward use the knife to clean up the residual stem from the body parts.

The adhesive usually recommended for assembling plastic kits is poly tube cement, but some modelers find it too thick and slow to dry. It also strings and can be messy. In my experience its properties can be improved by thinning with liquid

Plastic kits provide parts on runners, which need to be carefully separated. Use a sharp hobby knife over a cutting board, keeping the cut as far away as possible from the molded part to avoid damaging it.

Once the part has been removed, carefully trim away any residual plastic left from separating it from the runner.

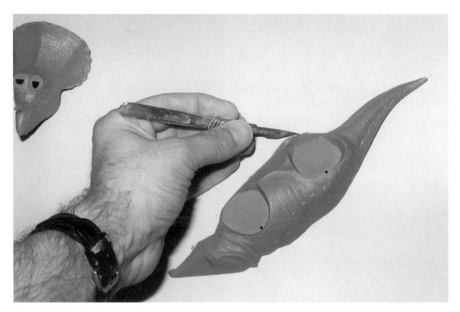

On many plastic kit parts, a seam occurs owing to the molding process. Here the flat of a craft knife is used to pare away the unwanted line.

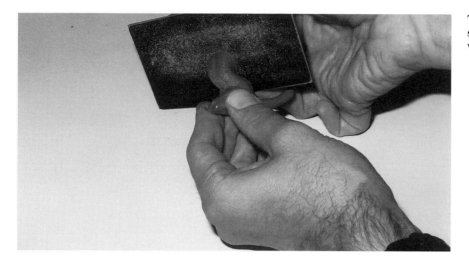

To achieve a cleaner fit between parts, sand the gluing (mating) surfaces flat with a Sandvik block, as shown.

Artist's masking tape (seen here) on Lindberg's raptor is helpful after gluing major parts, but bind halves tightly while the glue sets.

An alternative to tape for holding parts together is rubber bands. This Tamiya brachiosaur is firmly bound. In either case, allow tube cement to set hard. Leave it for at least 24 hours.

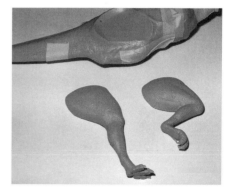

Complete all major subassemblies before joining them. Tamiya's *T. Rex* offers a choice of leg positions. Glue on the toes and claws first and remove seams by careful filling and cleaning up.

poly cement. The latter is sold in jars, and several brands are available, such as Testor's, Tenax, and Super Weld. These liquid polys must be applied by brush, but not a plastic one, since the cement will melt it. For a brush, I recommend a no. 1 sable with a wooden handle. Super Weld is fast drying and easy to use. Like all liquid poly cements, it actually dissolves plastic and when dry creates a welded bond that is extremely strong.

Having checked that the parts to be joined fit neatly, you can glue them together. If using tube cement, apply it sparingly to both mating surfaces before bringing them together. When using liquid cements, hold the parts together while using the brush to apply the cement along part of the joint; capillary action will cause the liquid to flow along it. Ensure that the cement has reached the full extent of the joint, wait ten seconds, then squeeze the parts together. You'll notice that melted plastic will ooze from the joint—don't touch it! It can be cleaned up later but only when the cement has fully dried.

On most major pieces, I use lengths of artists' masking tape firmly wrapped round the model while the glue sets. Rubber bands can also be employed. Don't attempt to clean up the joint line until at least 24 hours have elapsed: poly cement takes longer to set hard than many people think. Build up all the various subassemblies in the same manner and set them aside as recommended in the kit instructions.

SKIN CARE

There are various ways to clean up joint lines. My preferred method is still to use a sharp craft knife and gently run it up and down the line, paring away until

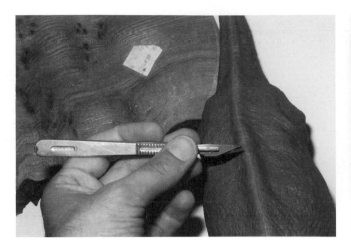

Once the glue seam has completely set hard, eradicate the joint line by careful scraping with a sharp hobby knife. Remove as little as possible of the surrounding plastic.

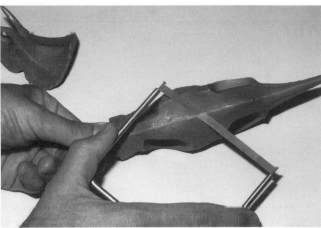

Another way to clean up plastic joint lines is with a Flexi-File, sanding gently at an angle from left to right. This versatile instrument gets in and around tight spots.

Use liquid poly cement for flooding between fine joints. Mix it to a thicker consistency with tube poly to seal slightly larger gaps before using filler as a final "top-up." Wear a mask or use adequate ventilation when working with all types of adhesive.

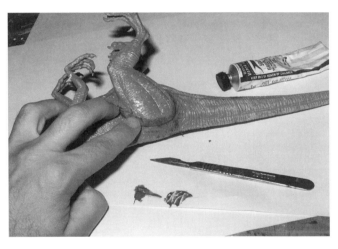

Squadron White Putty or Green Stuff are among the recommended fillers here. The latter is being smoothed into the leg body joint of a modified Lindberg raptor. Use water to thin the medium for easier application.

the plastic on either side of the joint is leveled. Sanding with carbide paper is not really recommended here because you are likely to remove too much of the surrounding surface detail, which will be difficult to restore. However, a Flexi-File can be used; also a motor tool—but with care. Remember if you use cement sparingly, there will be less of it to clean up afterward!

On Tamiya's dinosaur kits, the leg-to-body joints are usually good enough that little filling is required. This won't be the case with older plastic kits, however. Again I use tube cement to fix the parts, quickly followed by several brushfuls of Testor's liquid poly-

styrene cement to help fill the fine joint lines. Filling gaps on model dinosaurs is all important; after all, the main object is to create a creature that looks as though it is in one piece, with no gaps or breaks of line that belie its origins. I use Milliput or Squadron White Putty for disguising joints. Both can be thinned down with water, which is often a great advantage.

Milliput is produced in varying grades and may be found in art stores as well as hobby shops. Standard, white superfine, silver gray, and terracotta versions are available. All are excellent and have been used on most of the models featured in this book. Milliput is a two-pack medium; there are two lengths per box. Equal

Green Stuff has been used to fill large areas of the raptor's neck and head after surgery to close the open jaws. Leg positions have also been altered; hence, more filler.

Two-pack Milliput is a great filling medium. It, too, can be thinned with water, but dries rock hard and makes a good, strong adhesive bond. These Tamiya *Parasaurolophus* juveniles have had their limb positions changed, and all resulting gaps duly filled.

amounts are cut and kneaded together thoroughly between your fingers. If you have sensitive skin, thin rubber disposable gloves might be a good idea for this operation.

Milliput works only if the two mixed parts are of equal size and mixed properly until no streaking is visible. Follow the maker's instructions. Once it is mixed, Milliput sets rock hard and can be sanded, filed, drilled, and painted with ease. It remains workable for a couple of hours, slightly shorter if thinned with water. It's ideal for dinosaur modeling because it can be blended and smoothed when gap-filling to duplicate surrounding skin detail, thus keeping later sanding and reshaping to a minimum. We'll be returning to Milliput later.

In the case of very fine joints, such as inside mouths or between toes and claws, PVA white wood glue can prove effective when brushed into place. Capillary action will do the rest. Use water to thin it down and to clean brushes afterward. Use of a knife or Flexi-File to clean up dried filler later is recommended; but again, as with glue, the less you apply, the easier and quicker the clean-up. When the filled areas are dry, prime them with matte white or light gray paint. Nothing will reveal a poorly disguised joint better, and if necessary you can go over it again and again until all traces of your handiwork are rendered indistinguishable from the surrounding areas.

On some older, less well fitting kits (and there are many), a more drastic use of filler may be required. Sometimes you'll need to recreate the adjacent skin texture to eradicate a telltale seam or improve bare areas due to poor tooling or molding. Among the best products for doing this are Evans Prehistoric's specialized fillers aimed primarily at dinosaur modelers; they can be firmly recommended for resin and vinyl kits as well as plastic versions. They are extremely versatile. Wonder Putty is an ultrafine water-base filler that has the unique ability to retain both shape and molding impressions as it sets. Mix together the two elements, and after two to three hours, Wonder Putty is rock hard and ready to paint. It is designed to be used in conjunction with Evans' Repli-Scale, which precisely duplicates molded skin and texture detail.

Repli-Scale is another two-part medium that must be vigorously mixed in equal proportions. Use a disposable plastic spoon or spatula. You need to be quick, however, because this stuff sets in less than 60 seconds! To disguise dinosaur kit joint lines, quickly spread mixed Repli-Scale onto any convenient area of your model, pressing it firmly into the surface detail. After about five minutes remove the mold by gently rubbing it with your fingers. Hey, presto! You have a thin, "female" skin mold of the model's surface detail. Now apply Wonder Putty to the joint line and surrounding areas, smoothing and blending it in with wet fingers. Wait about 15 minutes until the putty is nontacky but still pliable; now press the Repli-Scale mold firmly into the putty surface for a perfect match.

I just wish these products had been available a couple of years ago when I started building the models for this book!

Teeth, claws, and horns are often poorly molded in plastic dinosaur kits. Unless you replace them entirely (as suggested in the next chapter), at the very least use a hobby knife to sharpen them up and remove mold lines before final assembly.

Improvements, conversions, extra detailing—none of these will prove too demanding when building plastic kits. These advanced techniques will be explained later.

RESIN KITS

There has been an explosion of resin-base dinosaur kits and models in recent years, and extensive constant-scale product lines from Kaiyodo, Lunar Models, The Dinosaur Studio, and others have provided the enthusiast with a large number of exciting and unusual subjects, many of which have never been available to modelers before. Resin kits are even easier to build than their plastic equivalents, but the appropriate adhesives differ, as

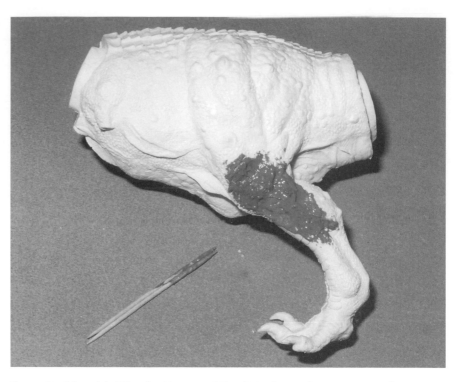

Evans Prehistoric's Wonder Putty and Repli-Scale products are great for dinosaur models. Molded skin impressions are easily formed with Repli-Scale. Simply mix it together, apply to the model, and when it is dry, peel it off. Easy!

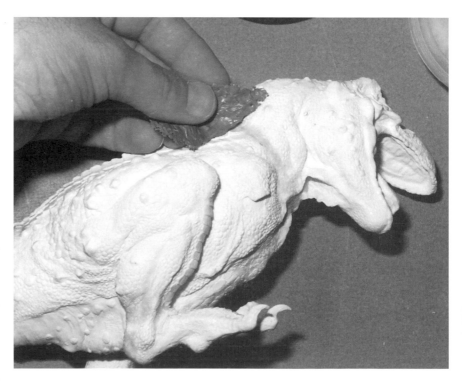

Having filled the gaps in this HAP *T. Rex* with Wonder Putty, leave for 10 to 15 minutes. Then press your piece of Repli-Scale into the semipliable putty to leave perfect skin detail matching the surrounding texture of the kit. Brilliant!

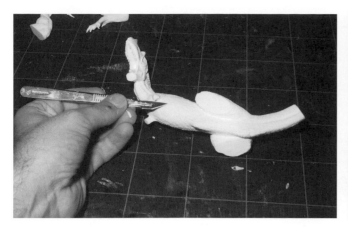

This Lunar Models' resin *Ceratosaurus* contains few parts, but each one requires careful cleaning up before assembly. The center seam on the one-piece solid body is removed by careful scraping with a sharp hobby knife. The flat gluing surfaces of the various parts await attention.

Sanding the mating surfaces of resin kit parts is essential. So is a face mask to prevent inhalation of dust. Mount the carbide paper to a solid, flat surface (a sheet of thick glass is recommended) and sand the part in a circular movement. Repeat for the various other mating surface areas on the body using a small sanding block or similar tool.

do assembly techniques. The American manufacturer Lunar Models quickly established a healthy market for its 1/35 scale product line of dinosaurs (sold as pairs or groups complete with diorama base), from masters sculpted by the gifted Bob Morales. Their *Ceratosaurus,* for example, is packaged with a *Stegosaurus* and baby and are typical of Lunar's series, as well as an ideal introduction to solid resin modeling.

There are generally fewer parts in resin dinosaur kits. Bodies are usually solid, leaving just legs, arms, jaw, and tail to add. However, even the best of them have centerline seams on most parts, sometimes faint, sometimes not, that must be carefully eradicated.

Once more, you can use the trusty modeling knife to great advantage, carefully paring and scraping away excess material that is normally softer than molded polystyrene and thus far easier to work. Major joints need more care. Usually you need to remove excess material from mating surfaces because of the casting process; and since this material can be quite substantial, use an X-acto saw, rather than a knife, to remove it. To achieve a really flat gluing surface, mount carbide paper to a smooth, hard surface with double-sided tape and gently grind the part to be glued in a circular motion until it's quite flat. Dust from resin can be dangerous if inhaled, so wear a mask or do all the sanding out of doors.

GETTING STUCK IN

The best form of adhesive for resin kits is any one of the various cyanoacrylate brands available on the market, such as Zap. If used properly, it forms an immovable bond. The real trick is to use only one or two spots on one surface, then apply the second part,

holding the two pieces together for a few minutes for the glue to grab. Afterward you can run more super glue around the joint or else use Milliput filler, which is almost as strong. The inexperienced user tends to flood the joints with cyano in the belief that the bond will prove greater, but, in fact, this only extends the setting time considerably. So use it sparingly!

Depending on the skill of the original sculptor, filling may prove to be minimal. Some artists carefully break down the parts around natural skin folds or muscles, but this is not always practical, so, again, you'll need the filler. Milliput is also ideal for resin kits and, once thinned with water, can be worked into the most awkward of creases or seams with a toothpick or old paintbrush. Lunar Models' own versatile fillers can again be recommended. Coats of primer are again mandatory to check your filling prowess. Most acrylics, enamels, and cellulose sprays can be used on resins, but always experiment on scrap pieces first if you're not sure.

Thankfully, resin can be carved, chiseled, and scraped quite easily with a good hobby knife or scribing tool. This can be useful if overzealous use of filler has clogged up molded detail. It can be easily restored, and you can also add more creases and scribe skin texture over filled joints to further disguise them.

Although display mounts and scenics are discussed later, it is sometimes a good idea to choose a base early on if only to have it to support the model while the glue, filler, or paint dries. Resin is easily drilled, and a short metal wire rod may be inserted into a leg, or two, and also into the baseboard as a temporary handling measure.

Sometimes flash is prominent on resin models, usually manifesting itself around smaller details, such as

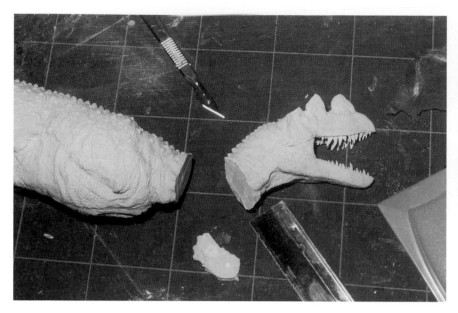

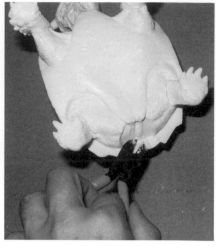

On large pieces of excess material in awkward places, use small wire cutters or tin snips to chew away the resin residue. Clean the molded piece later with a knife or file.

On resin models with excess material to be removed, don't use hobby knives, since the material is quite hard. Instead, use your X-acto razor saw and clean up later with carbide paper or files. This is the Monsters in Motion *Ceratosaurus* kit from an original sculpture by Tom Dickens.

Resin is easy to work on. Here a 1/20 Kaiyodo *Dilophosaurus* has its crests refined with a modeler's file. Dusting the file with talcum powder from time to time prevents clogging.

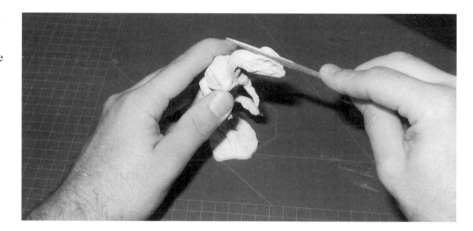

On large, heavy resin models such as this 31″ Saurian Studio's *Baryonyx walkeri* (from another Tom Dickens' master), reinforce all joints. I used lengths of wire coat hanger Zapped into holes predrilled with a power drill. Take care in aligning the drilled holes. At the same time, the foot may be similarly treated to provide firm anchorage to the base.

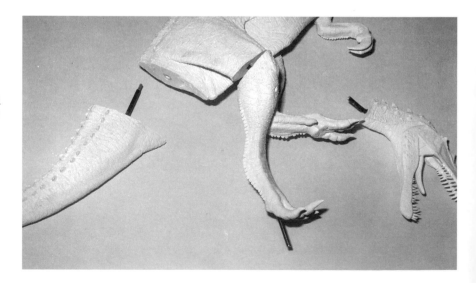

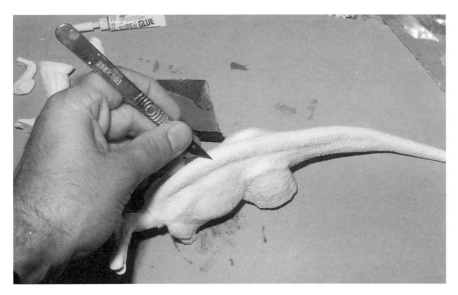

As with plastic kits, resin ones also feature seam lines that require removal. Because resin kits are softer, the scraping technique employed is easier to accomplish. Use the knife to rescribe skin wrinkles and creases across the spine. You can use a fine file as well for the same purpose. This is the Lunar Models' *Hypacrosaurus* resin kit (original sculpture by Bob Morales).

You can sand resin kits like plastic ones. Don't try this on vinyl, though! Smooth over the reworked *Hypacrosaurus* spine.

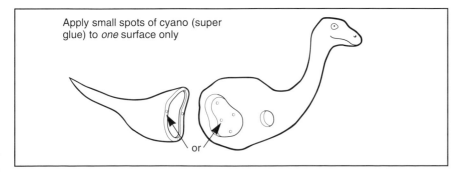

Apply small spots of cyano (super glue) to *one* surface only

or

teeth and spines. It can carefully be removed with a good hobby knife. But be aware that resin is quite brittle. You may damage smaller features if you are a little too heavy-handed.

VINYL KITS

A wide number of dinosaur kits have been produced in soft vinyl in recent years. Notable manufacturers include Kaiyodo, Horizon, and Tsukuda. The material is also widely used by those outfits producing SF and fantasy models, and it's hugely popular with many enthusiasts who prefer it over all other materials. Vinyl, because it is so soft, lends itself to easy modification, but that very property can often prove to be disadvantageous unless the modeler adopts certain precautions. Let me explain.

Vinyl softens considerably when warmed. Either submerge parts in a sink-full of hot water, or use an electric hair dryer to make them more pliable. Either way the vinyl will become floppy, making it much easier to trim off the excess material that all vinyl parts carry. Cut off the waste areas with sharp craft scissors or a hobby knife. When using the latter, have a cutting mat placed over the work surface and, as previously advised, always cut away from you. It is also far preferable to trim away too little material at first than to attempt to remove it all in one go. Don't use excess force when cutting; smaller knife blades, such as scalpels, can snap and send bits of fine metal hurtling into orbit. Protect your eyes—use goggles! If cutting does prove awkward, simply reheat the part and try again. Don't attempt to cut vinyl if it hasn't been softened first. Gluing vinyl kits together is not difficult. Either cyano or two-pack epoxy resin adhesives can be used. Sometimes I use both.

If the mating surfaces fail to match—and on some of the larger models they often do—heat up one

Use thinned-down Milliput or Green Stuff to fill joints, such as this neck-to-body subassembly. Use a toothpick to work the filler before it dries to carefully duplicate the surrounding skin-fold detail.

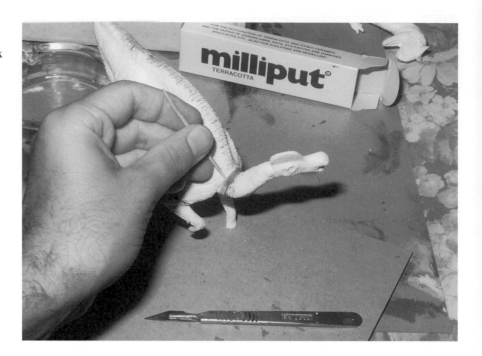

For small resin models, the base is sometimes cast integrally with the figure. This can be incorporated into your own base. The two are seen here glued with epoxy held by a G-clamp while it sets.

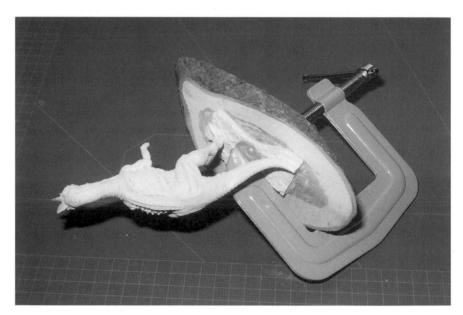

or both parts until they fit together properly, and glue together using spots of cyano. The gap-filling versions are ideal. They take slightly longer to dry, and once spread, will fill gaps quickly. Any excess can be removed when dry.

PROS AND CONS

As can be seen, the literal flexibility of vinyl can be a great asset when building model kits and when the heat-forming method is used to modify dinosaur models by changing limb positions, tails, etc. But once it has cooled, vinyl often tends to revert back to its original shape. If you want a stable model, glue lengths of stout wire (cut from an old coat hanger) inside the hollow parts to act as a crude but effective armature. If the model is a large one and stands on two legs, or even one leg, such as a *T. Rex* or raptor, it's a good idea to fill the leg or legs with plaster and allow to set hard before gluing to the body. This will also prove useful later if you are drilling into the leg for a wire stand support. Finally, don't display your vinyl models near domestic heating or boilers, under strong lights, or near a sunlit window even if you have internally reinforced legs and tails. Vinyl dinos don't like it!

FILLERS

Again, proprietary brands can be used. I favor Wonder Putty or

An assembled Kaiyodo *T. Rex* has been sprayed with matte white auto primer to highlight any glued or filled areas that may still warrant attention. Start over and continue until satisfied. In some cases, thick paint can disguise very thin gaps.

Before painting begins in earnest (see chapter 4), the model (Lunar's *Ceratosaurus*) is provided with a base undercoat color. In this instance, it's a pale yellow mixed from Pelikan Plaka water-base paints applied with a stiff brush. This will be one of the last chances to check whether your filling work has been done properly.

This Kaiyodo resin *Velociraptor* is an involved model that comes with its victim—a *Protoceratops*. The raptor's feet are molded to the prey, and thus the models must be preassembled and prepainted. Final filling is done at a late stage, necessitating careful cleaning and touch-up painting.

Temporarily mounting the model to the base helps when painting and doing other work. Resin is easily drilled to accept wire inserts or plugs and will make a stronger model when it is finally attached to the base. This is especially important if the model has only one leg in contact with the ground, making redundant the ugly external supports provided with some theropod dinosaur kits.

Typical content of a vinyl dinosaur kit. This is a 1/20 scale *Allosaurus,* one of Kaiyodo's impressive ongoing series of vinyl and resin models.

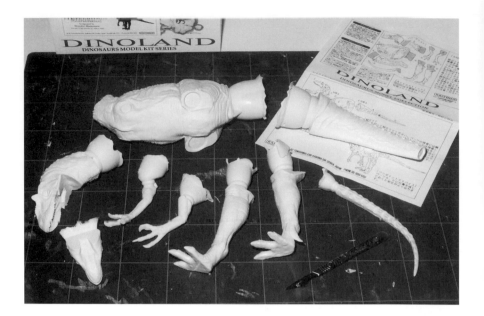

Separating excess material from vinyl kits is more easily accomplished if the parts are warmed up first with a hair dryer or by immersion in hot water. Take care when doing this and don't attempt to separate the excess material in one go. This is Horizon's *JP Dilophosaurus.*

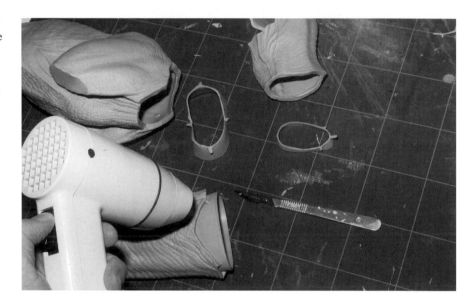

Use a sharp scalpel. It's better to separate excess material from vinyl kit parts in stages. Always soften the parts and wear safety goggles just in case. Knife blades do snap!

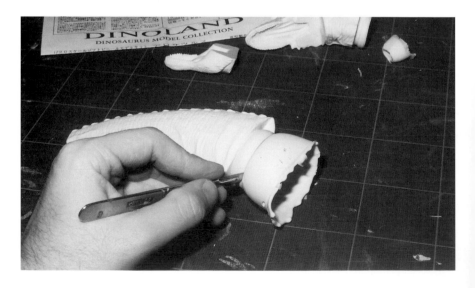

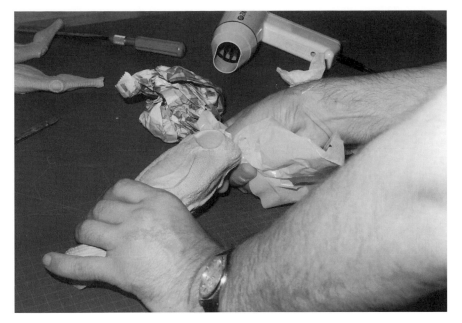

Get stuffed! On some vinyl dinosaur kits, the bodies are mismolded or distorted, giving a starved, pinched appearance. Heat the hollow body and stuff it with scrap material: plastic or paper bags, newspaper, etc.

Milliput, but two-pack epoxy glue can also be used in some circumstances to act as one of the strongest fillers around. You can thin it with water, which makes application quick, neat, and simple. On the Kaiyodo *Maiasaura* and *Camarasaurus* models featured in this book, both Milliput and epoxy were employed with equal success. Afterward use paint to prime the filled areas to check your work as before. Vinyl will take water-base and acrylic paints and even enamels, although many modelers don't recommend the latter because most oil-base paints will not dry out on vinyl and may even damage the surface. If in doubt, experiment first using the excess vinyl material previously trimmed off the model parts, as discussed above.

Application of a priming coat will also help to highlight holes present in both resin and vinyl kits as a result of air bubbles trapped when the parts were formed. These holes are usually quite small and easily filled; sometimes PVA white glue applied with a toothpick will suffice. Alternatively, glue small pegs cut from plastic toothpick tips in the holes using Zap or something similar. Simply let dry, trim off the excess stump, and sand flush. Another method for resin models is to add drops of gap-filling super glue into the hole until the adhesive stands proud. File or sand (or both)

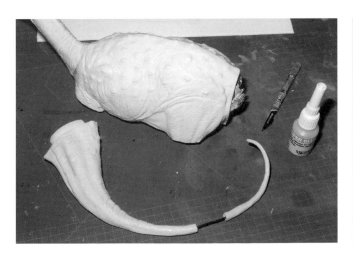

This Kaiyodo *Saltasaurus* body has been as fully stuffed as a Thanksgiving turkey. It's surprising how much you can get in. The stuffing prevents the vinyl, once cooled, from reverting to its original pinched-in appearance. Note soft wire insert to reinforce the tail joint.

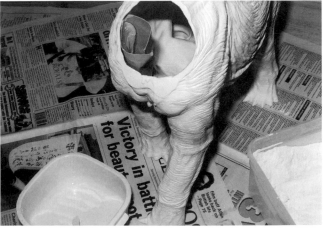

Another way to stabilize large models is to fill the legs with plaster, available from art stores. It is easily mixed with water. Apply it during assembly by using rolled-paper pouring tubes to reach awkward areas, such as seen here in a Kaiyodo 1/20 *Brachiosaurus*.

This Kaiyodo 1/20 *T. Rex* has had its body stuffed with waste paper while the head and legs are filled with plaster. When dry, the plaster can be sealed in with super glue. One can now drill the legs to accept mounting pins for displaying the model.

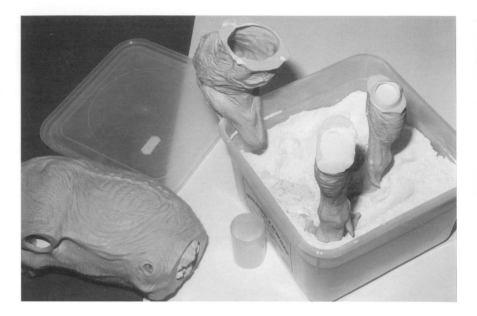

Using a sanding block is a good way of ensuring that mating surfaces are really flat before any gluing takes place.

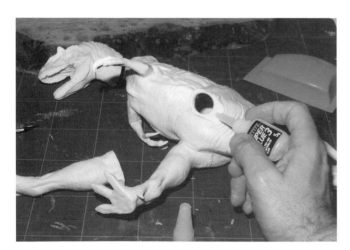

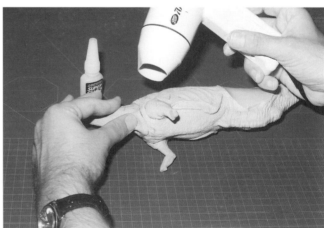

Use super glue sparingly. Only three or four spots around the periphery of one mating surface are required. Use gap-filling glue if you need a little longer to position the parts. Don't flood the joints.

Use hot water or a hair dryer when fitting vinyl kits together. Spot glue one side of the joint and heat the parts as shown. While the vinyl is still soft, match up the pieces, then spot glue to secure. This reduces the gaps and makes filling easier.

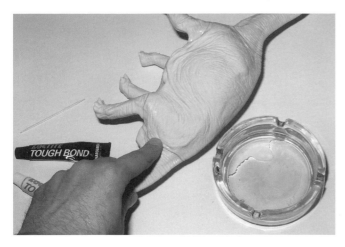

There's more than one way to skin a dinosaur! Here two-pack epoxy cement is used for gluing the neck, tail, and legs to the body. Later on, it can serve as a neat filling material in its own right. For a really smooth filling job that will require no further work, use water to dilute the epoxy before it sets. Run it into gaps to provide, when dry, almost invisible joint lines. The technique warrants practice. Wash your hands thoroughly after you've completed the work.

On this Kaiyodo 1/20 *Allosaurus*, thinned two-pack epoxy is being applied to the inner throat area with a cotton swab. Swabs are also great for cleaning airbrushes. The backs of open throats unavoidably have a joint line to eradicate, and a liquid filler is essential. You won't be able to sand this type of joint!

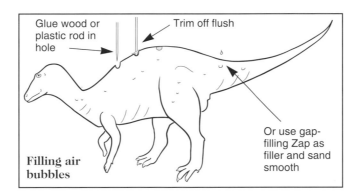

Glue wood or plastic rod in hole

Trim off flush

Filling air bubbles

Or use gap-filling Zap as filler and sand smooth

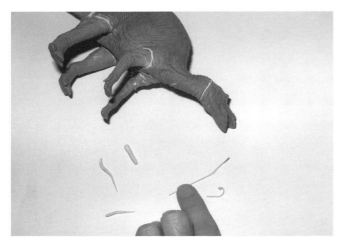

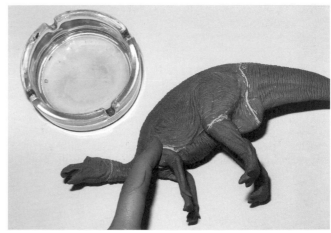

On Kaiyodo's 1/35 scale vinyl *Maiasaura* we see another method of joint filling. Use two-part Milliput thoroughly mixed and roll it out into very fine snakes. Apply these to the joints and press down between the joined parts with a toothpick before smoothing over with a wet finger.

Following from the previous photo: use plenty of water and rub the filler in well with your fingers, removing any excess from surrounding areas. If you have mixed up too much filler, repeat the technique to scratch build tree roots for the diorama base.

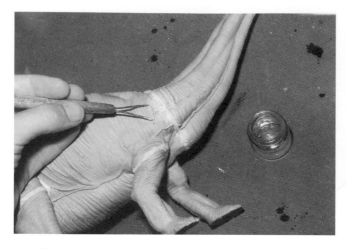

On different joints, the wet filler can be blended to match surrounding areas by using sculpting tools as shown. Take your time over this. It's not easy, but persevere. Practice!

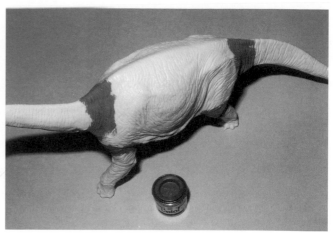

With the filler well dried, a coat of matte paint can be applied over the relevant areas as the usual check before applying the main color.

straight away, or within ten minutes, while the glue is still hard, but not harder than the adjacent resin.

Whatever type of filling material you choose, be prepared to spend a lot of time eradicating joints on model dinosaurs. Later we'll look at other techniques for dealing with them. Take your time and be self-critical. Nothing looks worse than an otherwise well-finished model with telltale seams, and this is especially so with figures and natural subjects. Be patient. And practice.

Once you are confident with your newly acquired skills, you'll want to go further and try changing basic kits, perhaps even converting them to other types of dinosaur. If so, then you must be ready for chapter 3!

On hairline joints, only minimal filling will be required. One neat alternative is to run PVA white glue for woodworking, thinned with water and applied by brush. Capillary action will do the rest. One or two applications may be required, however.

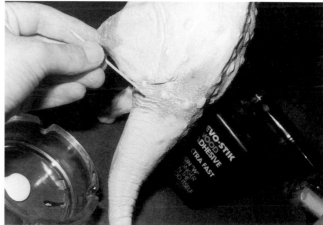

Test painting and drybrushing revealed imperfect joint filling. More filler was applied, and small warts and nodules were added from spots of PVA glue via a toothpick. Time-consuming but visually effective under a coat of paint.

3

COMING ALIVE

Once you have mastered the basic techniques of modeling dinosaurs from plastic, resin, and vinyl, you may find that the bug has really bitten and want to go further. Even the best kits require some refinement and correction. Changing the position of a neck, arm, leg, or tail gives the model an air of originality. Conversions are possible, and you can greatly improve teeth, claws, and eyes by using the simple techniques described in this chapter.

Plastic kits can be converted fairly easily. You can alter limb positions by cutting with a razor saw. You separate the limb at a natural joint, remove a wedge-shaped section, and reglue in the new position, later adding filler as necessary. Or you could saw part way through the limb, cutting and removing a wedge, then bending the limb forward to close the gap. The part may need gentle warming near its fulcrum to aid bending. A lit night-light or candle may be used. Hold

the plastic near the flame—not in it!

Tamiya produces some fine plastic dinosaur kits. Even though they provide a choice of parts in many of their models, simple and subtle alterations to head and leg positions will add a little originality.

Real dinosaurs are classified by paleontologists under various separate orders, and we can do no better than generally follow these groups. Each presents its own particular features, which need consideration when modeling them.

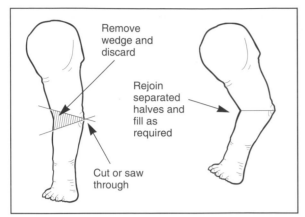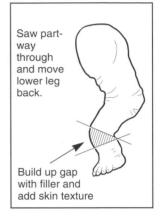

Panel 1 labels: Remove wedge and discard · Rejoin separated halves and fill as required · Cut or saw through

Panel 2 labels: Cut partway through leg and remove wedge · Gently heat fulcrum and bend halves together

Panel 3 labels: Saw partway through and move lower leg back. · Build up gap with filler and add skin texture

Three ways to change plastic kit legs

THEROPODS

Theropods were bipedal predatory dinosaurs with birdlike limbs and feet. Many were armed with sharp teeth as well as finger and toe claws. The various subgroups include *Allosaurus, Carnotaurus, Cerataurus, Dilophosaurus, Gallimimus, Tyrannosaurus,* and *Velociraptor.* Many will be familiar to moviegoers.

Understandably popular with manufacturers, theropods always make exciting subjects for modeling. Those teeth! Those claws! However, theropods pose a particular modeling problem—their legs. Few miniature *T. Rex's* will balance squarely on their own two feet, even fewer on one; they require extra support. Tamiya's *T. Rex* includes a metal rod, while some Horizon, Kaiyodo, and Tsukuda theropod kits provide a stand-mounted metal rod to prop up the model's chests. Few serious modelers would consider such an approach, although the metal post can be used for foot pinning.

Virtually all the models featured in this book have been incorporated onto some form of diorama base. This is a natural, power-sawed cross section of tree trunk or branch, which gives a more natural look than commercial stands and bases. The wood also doubles as a useful anchor for handling purposes. Simply drill a hole into the base and a corresponding one into

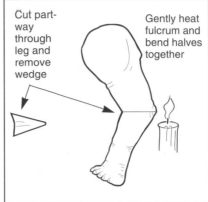

When converting plastic kits, such as this Tamiya *T. Rex,* you can use scrap plastic cut from the sprue trees, or scraps of plastic sheet glued together to serve as a base for filler. Once the glued plastic has set hard, apply filler over and around the area, blending and smoothing. Add surface detail to match surrounding areas.

You will need to support two-legged theropods such as Horizon's *Velociraptor.* Before assembly the legs were filled with plaster to serve as a firm bed, once drilled, for insertion and gluing of wire inserts.

If one of the legs is raised from the ground, you'll need to disguise the wire. Short lengths can be surrounded by groundwork material, but on larger models, small rocks or pieces of sandstone can camouflage the support. Here three pieces are glued around the wire and tucked neatly under the foot. You can cut and file sandstone, but it does shatter, so beware.

Rose thorns or similar objects may be used to make replacement teeth and horns for smaller models, such as this 1/40 Battat *Utahraptor*. Go for dead twigs and coat the thorns with super glue before cutting and trimming. This avoids the risk of splitting, and you will be able to sand them as well to blunt the tips.

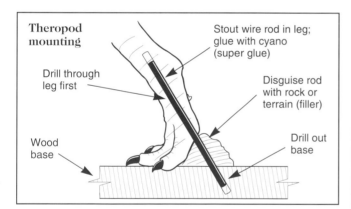

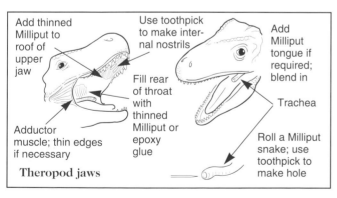

This *Gallimimus* is a Tsukuda vinyl. It was modified by heating the head with a hair dryer and cutting through the jaw line. You can then bend the jaws apart (as here), apply filler to the hollow areas, and sculpt detail. Use Milliput and don't forget the trachea, tongue, and internal nostril openings. Adding a ball of filler to the throat will determine the final jaw gape. You may need some extra filling around the base of the jaw when finished.

the foot-ankle-leg of the model. This requires care, since you don't want to drill too deeply and burst through the top part of the leg. Super glue can be used to attach the kit's wire rod support (which can be cut down using an X-acto metalworker's saw) to the model. Once the model is painted, and the diorama base semifinished (or before dressing, if desired), the two elements can be brought together.

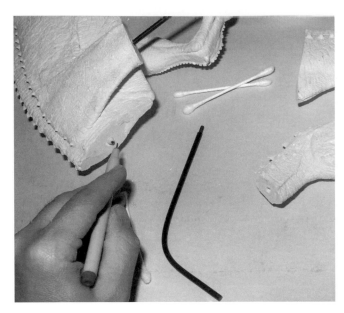

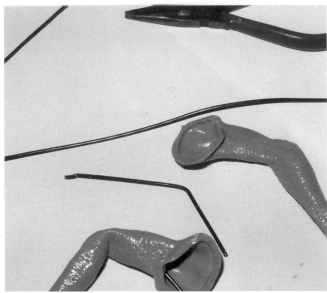

On large, solid resin models, which tend to be heavy, assembly may require some additional support, such as these lengths of wire for pegging the joints of this *Baryonyx*. Cotton swab tips colored with a pen aid alignment between joining surfaces, as described in the text.

Hollow vinyl models can be modified by heating with a hair dryer. In this way, you can alter limb positions. Once cooled, however, vinyl tends to adopt its original shape unless reinforced by pouring plaster or inserting wires. Coat hangers make ideal armatures for this purpose. However, when vinyl limbs are bent, the joints will crease and pinch in—not very realistic. Add filler and do a little sculpting work to build up the muscle shape.

Not surprisingly, most theropod kits are designed so that the jaws are agape, bristling with sharp teeth. The teeth are usually rendered well in vinyl, but resin versions will require careful cleaning away of the flash that invariably surrounds the teeth. In some cases, a few molars are missing altogether. All is not lost: you can make your own replacements. Milliput and Super Sculpey are ideal for making teeth, but the latter requires oven baking to harden the teeth. This material is used by many sculptors to produce masters and patterns, and we'll return to it later.

Whatever medium you select, roll out small amounts to the tooth size required. You should aim for a carrot shape. Flatten the elongated cone between finger and thumb, then bend to impart a curve. Leave to harden and be prepared to make a lot. For smaller models a simpler alternative is to use garden rose bush or briar thorns. Simply cut them from dead branches and trim as required.

Both techniques can be used to create claws as well as teeth. Teeth and claws can be prepainted before using tweezers for attaching them to the painted model. I use a toothpick to apply spots of super glue to the desired positions.

Few theropod models (or other dinosaur kit subjects) take into account the tongue, the trachea (windpipe) at the base of the tongue, or the internal nostrils

in the forward roof of the upper mouth. Milliput can be used to add all these features. Tongues are rolled out and flattened in a similar fashion to create teeth and claws. Tracheas are simply a rolled-out snake of Milliput. You can open the visible end of the trachea by pushing a toothpick into its center. For the nostrils, smooth a piece of Milliput into the roof of the mouth to build up a slight thickness, then use the tip of a toothpick to form a pair of slits before the filler sets. All these features can be done more or less at the same time. Use water and an old brush to blend them together and to blend around the rear throat area to disguise any visible joint line.

On very large resin theropods, such as Saurian Studio's *Baryonyx,* the sheer weight of the solid castings makes additional support of all joints essential. I used metal rods throughout, but they have to be aligned precisely, otherwise the outer edges around the mating surfaces will not align accurately. Use a cordless drill to make holes about 1″ deep in both neck and tail. Glue surfaces once dry and after removing any excess material and sanding the surfaces absolutely flat. Now drill corresponding locating holes in the front and rear of the mid-body section. Here's how to do it.

Use cotton swab tips cut to about 1″ long; push them into one hole until the woolen tip just protrudes. Wet the tip and dab it with a marker pen. Align the

Horizon's *JP* "Spitter" can be reconfigured to a more realistic *Dilophosaurus*. Obtain a good reference (these drawings are by Gregory Paul, from his excellent *Predatory Dinosaurs of the World*). Fill the interior of the head with plaster, then slice and trim off the molded crests—too large and too thick. When the head pieces are joined, lengthen the snout by adding Milliput to the nose and blending it in.

Lunar Models' *Carnotaurus* receives a new tail courtesy of a wire armature (or coat hanger). It is temporarily fitted then wrapped with tin foil to build up the rough shape.

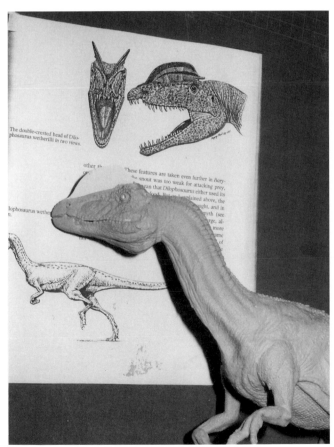

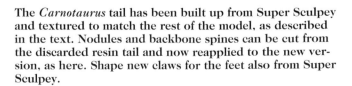

New crests are cut from .020 plastic sheet scored with a knife to provide surface detail. The two central vertical supports of each crest are simulated by brushing on ribbons of Kristal Klear. The crests are attached by using Milliput. Roll two thin snakes of the material and apply to the head using water. Press the crests into each ribbon and fair in with your fingers. When it is dry, reinforce with super glue. Note the remodeled, lengthened snout.

The *Carnotaurus* tail has been built up from Super Sculpey and textured to match the rest of the model, as described in the text. Nodules and backbone spines can be cut from the discarded resin tail and now reapplied to the new version, as here. Shape new claws for the feet also from Super Sculpey.

other part exactly and temporarily press together. This should leave a colored spot, which will indicate where to drill. Now remove the cotton swab. Test-fit the rod before gluing and make any necessary adjustments. Repeat for all other parts to complete the model.

Sometimes you may wish to correct errors on certain kits. This may include shortening or lengthening skulls, feet, or tails or cannibalizing parts from other kits to achieve different poses from those adopted by the standard kits.

On the Horizon *Dilophosaurus* model shown here, a lot of work was done to change the basic vinyl model of the *JP* "Spitter" to a more realistic version of the actual creature. This involved building up the snout after closing the jaws, removing the frill, adding an extra clawless finger to each hand, and replacing the head crests with larger plastic sheet substitutes detailed with pieces of Milliput (see photos for clarification).

The large 1/20 scale Lunar Models' *Carnotaurus* is a one-piece resin and well produced, but recent reference works indicate that the feet and toes are oversize and the tail too short. These are not uncommon problems. The feet, toes, and claws can be corrected by using saw and file to reduce their length and reshape them. The claws can be replaced with blunter versions made from Milliput. As for the tail, you can saw it off and insert—but don't glue—a piece of wire coat hanger, cut to the new length, into a predrilled hole.

Shape the new tail by wrapping and squeezing layers of aluminum foil over the wire to act as a base for the next material. You need to obtain oven-hardening polymer clay from a craft store. Fimo is one well-known brand, but Super Sculpey is recommended by most dinosaur sculptors who make patterns for vinyl and resin kits. One of these artisans is Bob Morales, who, along with Allen and Diane Debus, produced *Dinosaur Sculpting,* a book I can't recommend highly enough. Although sculpting dinosaurs from scratch is beyond the scope of this book, many of the excellent techniques Bob and Allen present can be adopted for kit builders, including building new tails.

The foil-wrapped *Carnotaurus* tail is covered by thin layers of polymer clay, shaped and smoothed with the fingers until its mating surface roughly matches the cross section of the kit body where the original tail was sawed away. The new tail, complete with its encased inner armature wire, can now be carefully withdrawn and baked in a domestic oven by following the instructions provided by the clay manufacturer. Once it is baked, remove the tail and leave it to cool. Next, press thin, rolled layers of Super Sculpey over the new tail. Surface detail matching that of the original model is then applied. How's that done?

SKIN DEEP

One of the most ingenious aids devised by Bob Morales in his book is the "texturing cup" (registered trademark of Dragon Attack!) for adding skin detail. By

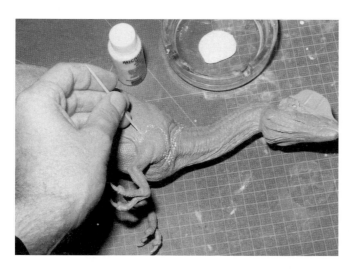

The converted *Dilophosaurus* has been primed with matte gray auto spray and is now being given extra skin detail. Use Kristal Klear to apply blobs as shown. Apply randomly with a toothpick, leaving small areas between each. When set, repeat the process by applying further blobs between the previous ones. It's time-consuming, but the result should be a pebbly skin. Reprime, then paint. If you think you still require extra pebbling, just add more Kristal Klear blobs.

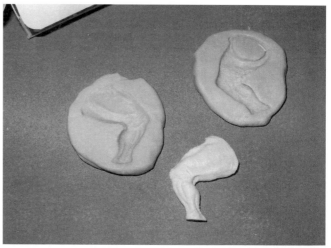

Use kit legs to make new castings Roll out two balls of Super Sculpey and flatten them out on a hard surface. Press the one-piece kit part into each halfway to provide two half molds. Bake the Super Sculpey according to the manufacturer's instructions.

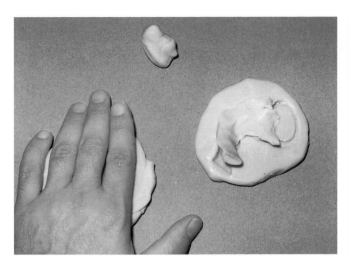

Coat the baked molds with super glue to seal them. Then roll up small clay pieces and push them into the leg molds and flatten. Remove any excess material squeezed out and flatten again.

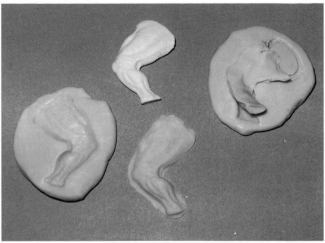

Carefully remove the new legs from the molds as shown, and you should have soft versions of the kit leg in two halves. In this photo, the original part is shown at the top.

slightly adapting Bob's process, we can use it for our kit models. Here's how.

Knead a piece of Super Sculpey into an elongated ball and press it anywhere onto the resin *Carnotaurus* body to leave a skin impression. Follow the maker's instructions and bake until it hardens. This becomes your "negative." Coat the skin area with super glue to seal it. When it is dry, push the glue into another, similar size piece of unbaked Super Sculpey to leave a raised impression. Bake as before, then seal with glue as before. This now becomes your texturing tool,

which matches precisely the skin texture of the model. By pressing this all over the new clay tail, you can achieve continuous, matching skin detail and render any joints invisible. The same method can be used on other kits to disguise large joint lines or blend in larger areas of filler as a result of major conversion. Of course, this whole process can be simplified by using Evans Prehistoric's versatile Wonder Putty and Repli-Scale to achieve the same result much more quickly.

If you feel really ambitious, you can adapt similar procedures for creating whole new limbs. First, take a

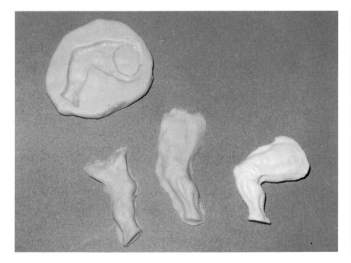

The two halves can now be carefully bent to their new shape (kit part at right) with minimal distortion, realistic stretching of muscle detail, and retention of skin detail. Bake the parts, file inner surfaces flat, and join together, cleaning up as necessary with your knife. Add filler as required.

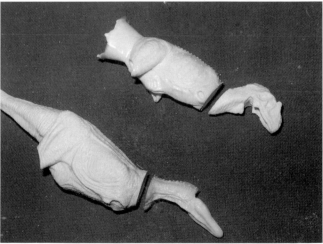

Another way to convert models is to swap limbs, tails, and heads between kits of a smaller scale. Here, vinyl and resin Kaiyodo allosaurs have switched heads. Simply saw apart, trim, and glue. Use filler to blend in the new joints.

On plastic kits, you can alter limb positions by sawing partially through an assembled part, removing a wedge, and bending the parts further to close the gap. Then glue. Or cut out a wedge, pull the halves apart, and fill the gap, as on this Tamiya *Brachiosaurus*.

Even ready-painted, one-piece models can be converted. This Kaiyodo *Kentrosaurus* has had all its joints filled, the tail spikes removed, and a new tail reshaped from Milliput. The forward spikes have been relocated to the hip area and the resulting holes filled. Recent study indicates that this conversion may be redundant, Kaiyodo correctly having the spikes in the original forward position!

kit part, say a straight *Triceratops* foreleg. You might want to bend it at both knee and ankle joints to give the impression the animal is at a gallop (spoiler alert: some scientists say horned ceratopsians couldn't gallop). Knead up two large molded lumps of Super Sculpey and imbed the molded kit part half way up its center line and flatten the surrounding clay. Remove, flip the leg over, and repeat the process using another lump of clay for the other side. Bake the two pieces. When they have cooled, seal the two impressions

you've made in the blocks (your female molds) with super glue and set aside to dry while you knead more Super Sculpey into a roll approximately the size of the original kit leg. Press it into one half mold. Repeat the process for the second mold. Press them firmly face down on a hard, flat surface; remove any excess Sculpey squeezed out from the sides of the mold. Flatten again. Now gently prize and peel the new floppy, copies of the kit leg.

The halves can now be carefully bent to the desired shape. Make sure they match. The original skin and muscle detail of the kit will be retained if you handle the pieces carefully. Once baked, the mating surfaces can be filed flat, then glued, and the joint can be cleaned up.

SAUROPODS

The next best known group is the sauropods. These were quadrupedal, herbivorous dinosaurs with long necks and tails and bulky bodies. They include *Apatosaurus* (or *Brontosaurus,* if you prefer), *Barosaurus, Brachiosaurus, Camarasaurus,* and *Saltasaurus.*

These make really impressive subjects, and anyone who has wrestled with Kaiyodo's massive 1/20 scale *Brachiosaurus* will know some of the problems they can present in assembly because of the sheer size of the pieces. You need a lot of room to build the biggest dinosaurs of all and a lot of room to display them. Dioramas may be out of the question for most modelers, unless they live in a mansion. Being four-legged browsers, sauropod models require little extra support if mounted to a base. However, when rearing beasts are modeled, you'll need those internal wire supports again.

The Kaiyodo *Barosaurus* resin kit is now hard to find but remains one of their best. Scaled to around 1/35, it is based on the awesome skeletal reconstruction displayed at the American Museum of Natural History in New York. It includes a juvenile, attacking *Allosaurus* and base. In this instance, not only did I use two wire pegs to stabilize the model's legs, but I added one to the tail for good measure. I drilled right through the tail into the base, glued the wire rod in place just below the surface of the resin tail, and plugged the entry hole with Milliput. All this done after painting, of course.

Only one, smaller pin was required for the baby *Barosaurus,* but this model was modified slightly by sawing along the jaw line and removing a wedge under the throat to achieve a gape. The inner surfaces were hollowed out with a hobby knife, and a scratch-built tongue from Milliput was added.

THYREOPHORANS

The thyreophorans were quadrupedal plant eaters. They include the plated *Stegosaurus* and the heavily armored *Ankylosaurus.*

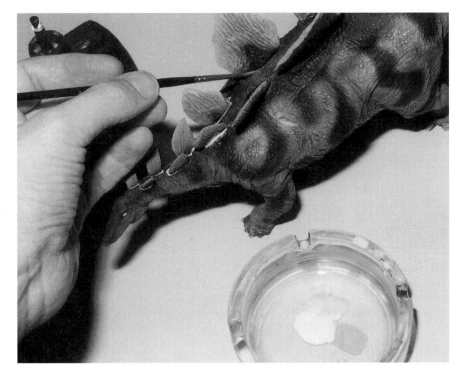

These *Stegosaurus* plates were pre-painted before they were glued in place. There will be gaps, and the neatest way to fill them is by brushing Kristal Klear or watered-down PVA white wood glue along the base of each plate. You may need to do this more than once.

The plated *Stegosaurus* makes a spectacular model, especially if you give those rows of back plates a vivid paint finish. Horizon, Lunar Models, and Kaiyodo all produce models of the popular *Stegosaurus,* and the latter, with its large 1/20 scale, is perhaps the most impressive of the trio.

Since the plates are the *Stegosaurus*'s most distinctive feature, they require care when fitting them. It is easier to paint the plates separately and install them at almost the last stage once the body has also been prepainted. After the plates are glued in their correct locations, you will probably find gaps all along their mating edges. These must be filled, best done using thinned-down PVA wood glue (use water). First, prevarnish the model and plates either by brushing or by spraying a flat clear varnish overall. Use a brush to run the PVA along the gaps; it should dry invisibly. Two or more coats may be required, but do leave at least 24 hours between them. When dry, revarnish.

The armored tanks of the dinosaur world were the large plated and spiked ankylosaurs. Kits of these are quite popular. Lunar's *Edmontonia* is typical, featuring separate shoulder spikes that are sharp. You'll need to be careful when building these dinos! The various spines and spikes usually carry a lot of flash on resin kits. This requires careful removal by scraping with a hobby knife. On Lunar's *Edmontonia,* the mold join line runs along the body below the spikes and is thus easier to remove by careful scraping.

ORNITHOPODS

The ornithopods were two- or four-legged dinosaurs with distinctive hip bones, stiff tails, and mouths designed for chewing plants. Among the subgroups of this classification are *Corythosaurus, Lambeosaurus, Maiasaura,* and *Parasaurolophus*—the so-called duckbills.

Tamiya produces an excellent *Parasaurolophus* and a juvenile version in its Mesozoic Creatures set, while Kaiyodo includes a 1/20 kit in its vinyl product lines. Several other duckbills are also available. Many recent published artworks restore *Parasaurolophus* with a web or crest behind its head, sometimes extending along the spine to the tail. The Tamiya model featured in this book has a web of plastic sheet, but when building the larger vinyl kit, I sought to replicate a more authentic-looking membrane. After some experimentation I came up with a workable solution.

The two Kaiyodo head pieces were "Zapped" together and left to set. I then heated the assembly with a hair dryer and used a knife to cut along and through the rear of the skull from the mating surface of the neck right round to the extreme tip of the skull crest. The cut is made on the centerline.

From here, follow the photos on page 38 to complete the crest. The result is worth all the effort. This method can be used for other types of models, as discussed in chapter 6.

MARGINOCEPHALIANS

Marginocephalians were herbivorous dinosaurs with a ridge behind the skull. Horned, thick-skulled, and parrot-beaked dinosaurs belong to

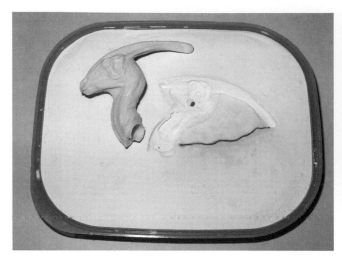

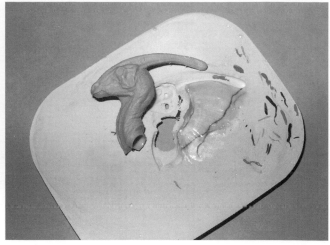

How to make a translucent membrane or web: Split the *Parasaurolophus* head centrally along the entire length of its rear edge then position in a tray before adding plaster to create a half mold. You can also achieve the same result using Super Sculpey.

Remove the head, sketch in the outline of the web, and apply four coats of liquid latex rubber, available in art shops for molding purposes. Allow at least one hour between coats. You can use a hair dryer to speed up the process.

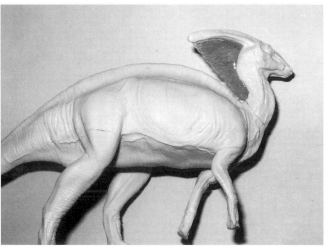

Once the fourth coat is dry, apply blood vessels (red) and bundles of nerves (purple) with a really fine brush. Thinned enamels are best, since latex can smudge water colors. When it is dry, apply four more coats of latex.

Remove the web, prize open the rear of the skull, and trap the inner edges of the skin between them. Secure with super glue. Any gaps can be filled with Kristal Klear. When airbrushed lightly in the chosen color, the veins and arteries will still be visible. The result is extremely convincing.

this broad group. Among the varied subclasses are *Stygimoloch, Anchiceratops, Chasmosaurus, Pachyrhinosaurus, Protoceratops,* and *Triceratops.*

The thick-headed pachycephalosaurians are poorly represented in the dinosaur model world, which is a shame because they were spectacular creatures and deserve a wider audience. At the time of writing, I am aware of only one large model produced in recent years. This is *Stygimoloch,* a one-piece resin model to 1/5 scale from an original sculpture by Mike Jones and marketed by Saurian Studios.

One-piece resin dinosaur models are gaining popularity. Several U.S. manufacturers produce them for collectors; they are available painted or unpainted. They are usually to quite large scales and not cheap, but then they are aimed at a slightly more specialist custom base than that for plastic and vinyl kits.

Generally, there are few seams to remove with the best of these models, although air holes are common. Since we've already dealt with curing these problems, there's no point in discussing them again. In the case of the *Stygimoloch,* one of the feet is cast integrally with

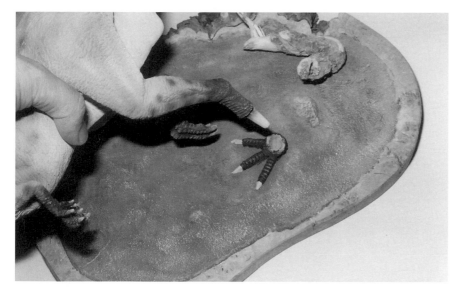

On some resin kits (this is Saurian Studio's *Stygimoloch*), the model is designed to stand on one foot by having the leg terminating in a peg and the foot cast into the base. This is okay, but I still added a wire insert for extra insurance. You'll have to paint the model before gluing to the base, which makes any filling and retouching a little more tricky than usual.

This is Lunar Models' *Pachyrhinosaurus* pair. These two resin models are being converted by an exchange of heads. You'll need to saw off some extra pieces of neck to ensure the new mating surfaces match more closely and thus reduce the amount of filler required.

The nasal horns as molded were cut down with a razor saw and some of the smaller forehead spikes removed. Others were reshaped with a hobby knife.

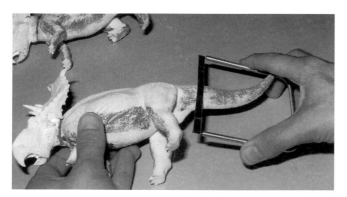

Once all the corrective work has been done, the heads and tails swapped and joints filled, the models can be cleaned up. The Flexi-File is useful here, since it can cope with compound curves very easily as well as reaching the most awkward areas.

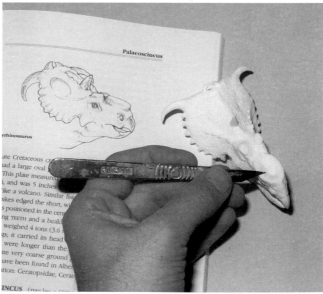

Here a knife is used to resculpt the resin nose area to provide a dished stump. Resin is great material; you can easily carve and score it to make new shapes. Because resin is soft, such tasks are not arduous.

the base and slotted to accept a peg that is part of the leg. It makes a reasonably strong joint, but I wouldn't rely on this alone. Drill out both pieces and fit a wire insert, as previously described.

REFERENCES

If you are serious (well, not *too* serious!) about dinosaur modeling, you should invest in some good reference books to help you. There are a lot of dinosaur books out there, but I would recommend only a few for our purposes. The bibliography lists those that I consider to be the most reliable and that I have used in pursuing my hobby and preparing this book. Most useful are those that provide accurate side elevations of skeletons and surrounding tissues.

One artist and author, Gregory S. Paul, is the answer to a dinosaur modeler's prayer. Not only does he execute superb side views of dinosaurs, he also provides top and sometimes front views as well! Since Mr. Paul is also interested in airplanes, I suspect he may have some sympathy with modelers. Certainly the images in his classic book *Predatory Dinosaurs of the World*

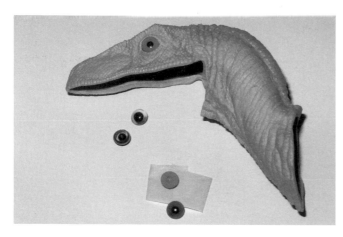

I employed teddy bear eyes to improve Horizon's 1/30 raptor. The flat, inner surfaces of the plastic eyes had their centers drilled and painted black. The whole surface is overpainted pale green with dark green detail.

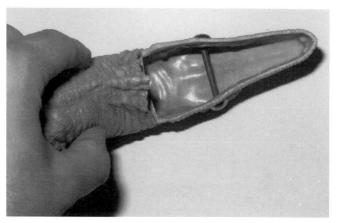

On hollow vinyl models, a plastic rod brace glued between the eyes prevents them from being accidentally pushed back into the model's interior.

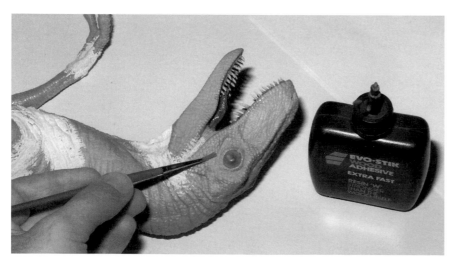

You can mask eyes with Kristal Klear or PVA white wood glue before painting. Once the model has been finished, insert the tip of a scalpel under one edge of the eye and pop off the dried, clear skin. Reapply Kristal Klear around the periphery of the eye.

Prepainted glass eyes are available from taxidermy outlets. You can also obtain clear versions you can paint yourself. However, wide ranges of colors, styles and sizes are available, so there's plenty of choice. Simply drill out the eyeball area and test-fit the new eyes.

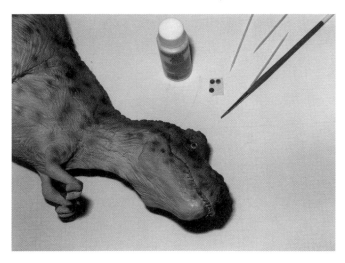

This Bill Wieger *T. Rex* has already had its molded eyeball drilled before priming. Paint the socket deep rose red, leave to dry, clear varnish, then apply a blob of Kristal Klear with a toothpick. Now drop in your glass eye. It doesn't matter if the Kristal Klear oozes out, since it dries invisibly anyway. Later, if you want to suggest weeping, gloss varnish can be applied around the eye and below it.

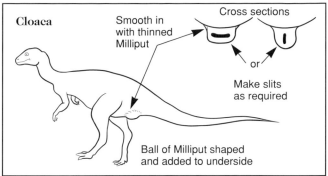

reflect the approach taken by many writers of airplane monographs. Some of Mr. Paul's art also appears in Don Lessom and Don Glut's *Dinosaur Society Dinosaur Encyclopedia,* another work I would recommend.

Good technical reconstructions are extremely helpful to modelers. If you have access to a xerox machine with enlarging facilities, you can make copies for your own use to the size of the model you are building and check it for accuracy.

All the above assumes greater relevance if you are interested in modifying older kits, converting and adapting more recent ones in line with the latest researches, or creating full-blown dioramas. Sometimes the experts disagree, not only on the lifestyles and interrelationships of dinosaurs but on their appearances, too. Certain sauropods may have had a row of spines along their backbones, ankylosaurs may have been far broader than originally thought, and *T. Rex* is no longer the largest predator ever to have walked the Earth.

The *Pachyrhinosaurus* models featured here are a case in point. Some artists show them with blunt nasal stumps on their foreheads; others depict these ceratopsians with enormous nose horns and extra spikes around the frill. The latter configuration is that adopted by Lunar Models' 1/35 pair from masters sculpted by Bob Morales.

For the featured models, I decided to adopt configurations based on earlier researches and so removed the nasal horns and extra head spikes. To change their appearance even further, I exchanged the models' skulls and did the same with both tails, using Milliput to fill any resultant gaps. Then I restored the surface detail using the previously described skin-texturing

methods. Alternatively, you can apply small beads of PVA wood glue or Kristal Klear to add scaly nodules. This is time-consuming, but effective nonetheless.

There's one other anatomical feature that some dinosaur manufacturers forget—the cloaca. What's that? The cloaca is a combined outlet for natural body wastes, sperm, or eggs. Most recent reconstructions show it just behind the legs and before the start of the tail. Tamiya kits include the feature, as do most Kaiyodo models; but if it's missing from your dinosaur model, a ball of Milliput can be used to form a small lump under the model at the tail's base. Use a toothpick to form a small slit (either vertically or horizontally) and blend the filler into the surrounding area, adding matching wrinkles and skin texture as necessary.

You can use the toothpick should you wish to enlarge the orifice and simulate the ejection of Milliput eggs or less attractive, but equally natural, bodily products. These features would add greatly to the realism of any diorama scene; after all, we are trying to replicate living creatures—warts and all.

EYEBALL TO EYEBALL

As with any figure model, the eyes are naturally the focal point, and this is just as true for dinosaur miniatures. These can be painted on smaller replicas (see chapter 4) or else replaced with glass eyes, available either painted or unpainted from taxidermist suppliers. These plastic eyes are available in a bewildering number of painted styles and different sizes. Those for birds and reptiles would be the most appropriate for dinosaurs and can look extremely effective. There are several ways of mounting them, and each demands care in handling. Use only SuperScale's Kristal Klear to attach them after the model is painted. Why Kristal Klear? First, it won't harm paint or varnish. Second, it sets slowly and gives you plenty of time to position the eyes. It also dries invisibly. You can also use it as a filler around the eyes later, if required, or as a false eyelid, or even as a masking fluid if overspraying the model. It's a highly versatile medium, and more modelers should make use of it.

4

COLOR THE BEASTS

Since no one has ever laid eyes on a real, live dinosaur, no one knows what colors they were. Not the most highly respected paleontologist, nor you, nor me. What a pleasant experience to enter a model contest confident in the knowledge that neither judge nor nitpicker can accuse you of an inaccurate paint finish. You don't have to worry about decals, either!

It's possible most dinosaurs were light colored underneath and dark above. Mottled patterns may have characterized medium herbivores living in forest areas. Predatory types may have been brighter, while frilled and sail-backed dinosaurs, or those with crests, may have boasted really vivid colors to enhance their display. Bright "plumage" serves several purposes: to attract mates, to warn off predators, to threaten rivals—all adaptive. Large adult sauropods' very size protected them from most predators, so perhaps camouflage was unnecessary. But because of these dinosaurs' enormous skin area, darker shades may have been normal for protection under the sun. But all this is pure hypothesis. We'll never know, and that's what makes painting model dinosaurs so exciting, so much fun.

PRIMED

We are discussing three kinds of model kits in this book—plastic, resin, and vinyl. Most newcomers will ask, What paints are best to use on all types? Enamels work well on plastic and resin, but not on vinyl. Water-base paints such as acrylics work well on vinyl and

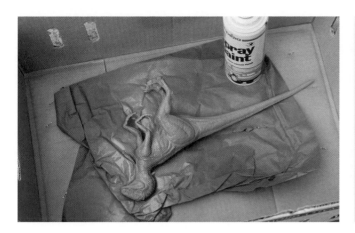

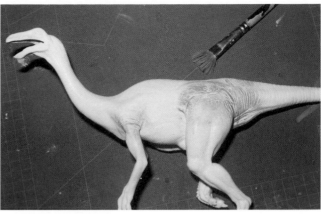

For an ideal surface on which to apply almost every kind of paint finish, spray your model with auto cellulose aerosol primer. It is available in at least four matte colors. The primer will seal the surface and soon reveal any imperfect areas that should be attended to before respraying.

Once the surface is primed, you can really check your filling work by drybrushing in water colors. If this reveals missing areas, or the joint line still remains visible, refill, reshape, and redetail as necessary. Wash off the water colors and reprime. This work is important. Do it now before you apply your chosen color scheme.

plastic but not so well on resin. You can solve all these problems in one stroke by priming the models first, after washing to remove grease, etc.

One of the most versatile primers is the cellulose auto spray primer, which can be used to provide an even, flat, virtually matte surface that accepts all types of paint. It is available in white, black, gray, or red oxide. Two lightly dusted coats from the aerosol can are usually all that's required, but do follow the maker's directions on the canister and allow plenty of time between applications. I'd also advise spraying cellulose outdoors in still air, and use a disposable face mask to avoid inhaling the vapors.

Cellulose spray not only provides a superb base for painting but will soon reveal any imperfections and poorly filled areas that will need attention before painting. This is important. Study the model critically and attend to these areas to your satisfaction before starting to apply the final color scheme.

My preferred paints are water-base ones, and I tend to use those casein emulsion colors produced by Pelikan Plaka of Germany. These are favorites with many figure modelers. I've been a fan of these paints for years, not only for models of all kinds but for airbrushed artwork, too. Plaka paints mix easily with water and cover well. The colors are solid, they can be overpainted with ease, dry matte, and are great for airbrushing when suitably thinned. They are also waterproof when fully dry. All these features offer great advantages, and being almost odorless as well, the paints won't offend other, nonmodeling members of your home.

When you consider that the painting of any scale model is often the most demanding and time-consuming aspect of modeling, it is surprising that relatively few tools are required. It is false economy to purchase cheap tools, whether airbrushes, spray guns, or other types of accessories, brushes especially. Your first move is to obtain a varied selection of good quality sable or nylon brushes, and these should be acquired from an artists' supplier who stocks only the very best.

Although sables and nylons are expensive, if properly looked after, they will outlive most other types of brushes because the bristles are somewhat more resilient. The size of the brush is also important. Surprisingly, it is not always the case that the 0 or 00 size is the best choice for very small details. A good no. 2 sable with the tip slightly dampened before painting often gives superior results, since the larger bristle is easier to handle. Sizes ranging from 00 to no. 10 would cover most needs, with perhaps one or two fine-lining, chisel, or stencil brushes to complete the selection.

However many brushes you have, you'll need to look after them properly both during and after use. No brush should ever be used to stir paint, since nothing will remove the hairs more quickly. Neither should any one brush be used for all jobs. Each ought to be reserved for particular applications and marked clearly as such. Never leave the brushes to soak in thinners—or water either. Clean them thoroughly, then wipe them on a clean, soft, lint-free cloth. If you are using the same brush for different colors, you should have three small bottles filled with water or thinners at hand. Use the first to get most of the paint from the brush, the second to rinse, and the third as a final dip before carefully wiping. To protect the hairs afterward, use a short length of plastic tubing slipped over the metal shank. Many artists' brushes are available with

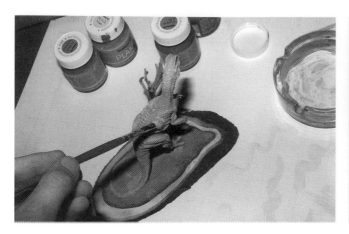

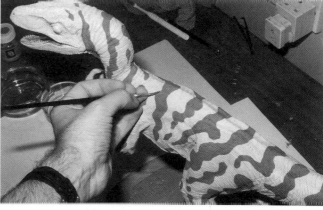

This small Kaiyodo resin *Dilophosaurus* has been mounted to a new base and had a Milliput tail added to it. The plinth also serves as a useful handhold. An overall ocher has been applied. Drybrushing the molded detail with a lighter version of the same color, just catching the high spots, will highlight the ocher. You can add secondary colors next, then drybrush these in appropriate paler shades.

This Horizon raptor has already been given an ocher undercoat drybrushed with pale ocher to highlight the molded detail. Now it has rusty brown camouflage stripes added with a fine brush. The darker segments can later be drybrushed over, using a paler brown. A smaller, flat-edged brush will be required for this.

these ready fitted, but alternatives are easily found in the form of model airplane neoprene fuel tubing. This can be bought in various diameters and chopped up to provide durable sheaths. Finally, the brushes should be stored in an airtight container, such as an old pencil box. Never store them upright or leave them standing in a jar.

APPLICATION

Generally, it's best to apply the lighter colors first (usually on the belly area), then a medium shade on the legs and flanks, and finally a darker finish on the extreme upper surfaces. Newcomers will find that good results will be obtained if the chosen colors are of a similar shade: pale green, medium green, and dark green, for example. The medium green can be a standard, ready-mixed color; and by mixing white and black with it in separate jars or palettes, you can achieve the desired, varied shades.

Remember that paints take time to dry, and many a model has been spoiled by a lack of patience. Paints of most types touch-dry quickly as the solvent evaporates, but other constituents in paints, such as hardeners, will take longer. I'd recommend at least 24 hours before recoating. If applying water-base paints or enamels by brush, the techniques are the same, except that different cleaners and thinners will be required to suit. Always choose matte/flat paints. These are easier to work with, grab the surface detail better, and dry a little faster than thicker gloss enamels and acrylics.

More elaborate color schemes are limited only by your imagination, once you have got the hang of painting. Finer brushes can be used to create streaks of contrasting shades or blotches, and mottling can be applied with a stiff, flat-tipped brush or with small pieces of foam or sponge dipped into the paint.

BRINGING OUT THE DETAIL

There are various ways to make your model look even more realistic. These involve drybrushing for highlighting techniques, the application of washes, and weathering with pastel sticks.

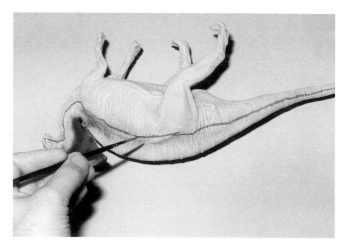

Painting *Parasaurolophus*. The latex web has already been airbrushed in scarlet and its outer edges in purple over the highlighted gray beige base color. The back of the beast is painted in three bands of irregular color, following a scheme used on several paintings by British paleoartist John Sibbick. Red ocher is applied first, then yellow ocher, and finally purple, which blends into the presprayed head areas. For highlighting various colors, one overall pale shade won't do. Each individual color must be drybrushed with a lighter shade to match. Just mix white with the three chosen colors and use a small brush to do the job.

The Tamiya *T. Rex* has been airbrushed with Pelikan Plaka. The result is a pale fawn belly, light red brown sides, and dark red-brown-black upper areas carried down the sides in vertical stripes. Drybrushing techniques highlight the skin texture with lighter versions of all the above three colors applied to the relevant areas.

If you don't have an airbrush, you can still achieve some spectacular results with drybrushing techniques. Two shades of green have been applied to this Lunar *Hypacrosaurus*. The sharp division lines between the brush-applied colors can be softened by drybrushing in a medium green shade. Practice the technique. Use different contrasting colors and experiment. You can use small pieces of foam sponge to apply the paint and create easy, soft-edged patterns.

Drybrushing is fairly easy and works well on those dinosaur models with heavily molded skin texture. Once the model has received its base coat (we'll stay with green) and been left to dry for a day or so, mix up a lighter version of the green with pale yellow. Now dip the tip of a medium, flat-tipped nylon brush into the paint and wipe it on scrap card or white paper until only a hint of the paint remains. Now work the brush quickly over the model. If you are careful, the lighter color will catch only the raised detail, leaving the base green intact, and thus impart a pleasing depth to the surface. You can use white to lighten colors, but I

rarely make use of pure white or black as finishing colors on my models.

Another effective way to highlight the skin texture is to first prime or paint the model overall in black or matte black, and leave to dry. This is your "skin shadow." You can now paint the entire model by drybrushing—lighter colors beneath, darker ones on top.

On my Kaiyodo *Styracosaurus*, I undertook successive sessions of drybrushing upper areas with dark umber, then red brown, red ocher, orange, and yellow. I allowed plenty of drying time between all the

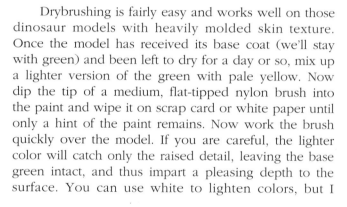

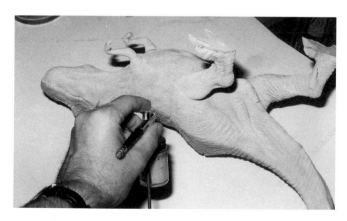

If airbrushing, spray the lightest color first, usually on the underside of the model. Do the sides with the next lightest color (pink here), then use a dark brown mottle, followed by a much darker one over the very top of the head, back, and tail. If you're not happy with the first attempt, try again (see the caption to the next photo).

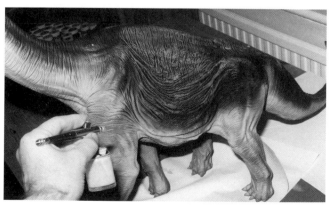

On my *Brachiosaurus*, a second application of colors was more satisfactory. A less obvious mottling with fewer spots looked better. Colors are Pelikan Plaka water-base paint over auto matte white primer.

colors. The trick is not to let the colors mix, and with careful, patient drybrushing, this can be avoided. The result should be a colorful, toned appearance, leaving the original black undercoat between all the skin folds and wrinkles.

WASHES

To achieve a similar sense of depth and shading, you can adopt an alternative method using washes, as the accompanying photos show. Apply a base color on the undersides; for example, cream or light beige. To avoid possible removal of the base color (much less likely if the paint has fully dried), coat the underside with a clear matte varnish. When dry, mix up a weak solution of water and raw umber and apply liberally to the undersides. Use a thin tissue to wipe off the paint, wiping in one direction only, which leaves the darker pigment settling into every crevice, crease, and fold. The molded wrinkles and scales will now become more apparent. Another way to achieve the same result

is to apply the base color as before, but mix a little raw umber with matte varnish to tint it. Brush lightly over the model, and the creases will be filled while the overall base color becomes slightly darker.

Kaiyodo and Dinosaur Studio models are so well sculpted that drybrushing may not be required; washes work well with these. On plastic kits such as Tamiya's *T. Rex* and *Triceratops,* drybrushing techniques are more effective because of the way the surface detail is molded, but thin washes may also be used.

If you're not happy with the first attempt, simply paint over the original pattern until you achieve the desired finish. Once the model has been painted to your satisfaction, it may then be clear varnished overall.

AIRBRUSHING

Airbrushes are considered luxury items by many new modelers, but can provide some stunning finishes once the required skills to use them are mastered. Detailed airbrush techniques fall outside the scope of

This shows the stages in painting *Maiasaura*. After priming with matte dark earth enamel, paint the undersides with Pelikan Plaka, or similar. In this case, I selected a light beige and left it to dry.

Now for another method of highlighting detail. The water-base Plaka base coat is fixed with clear polyurethane varnish. Satin is best. Allow plenty of time for it to dry.

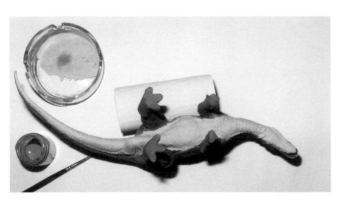

Next, mix up a thin solution of dark brown and black water color. Using a full brush-load, apply liberally to the model's underside.

With a lint-free cloth, wipe along the model in one direction only. The dark wash should remain in the crevices and folds of the molding for a most pleasing effect. Repeat until the desired depth of color highlighting is achieved.

You can further enhance skin folds by using a mixture of watered-down raw umber and black. Apply it directly with a small brush before drybrushing. Capillary action should help the thin paint to flow along the creases and folds, adding depth.

Here's another, quicker method. Paint the model in the desired color, ensuring that the surface is matte. Apply artist's pastels to the model. This medium, especially when integrated into a diorama base, is very effective for giving the impression of sand and dust on the model's belly and legs. The pastels may be fixed later with a clear spray fixative.

You'll find aids for holding parts and models most helpful when painting dinosaurs, especially when trying to finish complete lower and upper areas, where your hands may get in the way. This converted Kaiyodo *Allosaurus* is securely clamped while the mottled finish is applied.

this book, and I would refer readers to our sister title, *Painting and Finishing Scale Models*, by Paul Boyer, for detailed clarification of both operation and application. So although it's by no means essential to use an airbrush for finishing dinosaur models, it can prove an excellent addition to your tool kit and perhaps deserves more than a passing mention here.

Not all the models featured in these pages were completely airbrushed; but for mottling effects, subtle shading, even weathering, my trusty Badger 200, really came into its own. If you have never tried airbrushing, it's well worth reading up on techniques. Practice and more practice will be the eventual key to success.

Simply put, the essence of trouble-free airbrushing is rigorous cleaning of the equipment, coupled to the right consistency of paint and exercise of restraint by applying the paint slowly and gradually. It's not really necessary to rely on the airbrush for entire, overall finishes. I've obtained pleasing results making partial use of the tool with light mottle effects over a completely brush painted model, for example, or adding a few contrasting horizontal bands or stripes of colors. Alternatively, you can initially restrict airbrushing to applying dust effects around dinosaur feet and over surrounding diorama areas, while you gain experience and confidence.

Air compressors to power your airbrush may seem yet another expensive purchase, but I do advise you to invest in one. Aerosol canisters are a poor substitute and offer scant value for money. They don't last very long, and it's often difficult to regulate the air pressure, especially when they are near empty. The total outlay of several cans would be far better put toward a compressor.

The Pelikan Plaka paints I favor work extremely well through airbrushes when suitably thinned with water. The thinning should be done properly. The correct consistency should be such that a droplet of paint placed on a vertical glass surface (like the inside of a paint jar) runs down freely, leaving a strong trail of color.

I recommend an F (Fine) nozzle setting for airbrush work on most dinosaur models. Hold the airbrush at least 3″ from the model surface and keep it moving. Practice on scrap paper or card first. For mottling dinosaur skin, you can fire small bursts at the

Stegosaur plates demand care. On Horizon's 1/30 vinyl scale kit, the separate plates are singled out with toothpicks, which hold the parts during painting, and tags as identification. Once the vinyl plates are removed from their base molding, unless they are tagged, it will be difficult to tell many of them apart. None is identical.

On this vinyl Kaiyodo *Stegosaurus,* we use another method. Spray the plates before cutting them from their molded bases. The plates are first painted crimson overall, then drybrushed pale pink. Spray the edges yellow ocher and the centers very dark brown. Both secondary colors are then drybrushed in appropriate lighter shades.

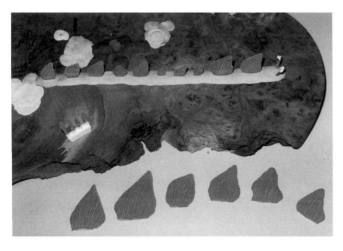

On Lunar's resin *Stegosaurus,* the molded number tags will probably fall off during transit, making identification time-consuming. If there are no slots to insert handholds and few molding stems, you'll need to steady the parts while painting. Use a roll of plasticine and press it to a hard surface before pushing in the plates. About 1/8″ depth will be okay. Not only will this hold the parts during painting, but the gluing area will be untouched, making cleaning up of mating surfaces unnecessary.

Before leaving the subject of airbrushing, I would like to summarize the most important points you should remember:

1. Choose a recommended brand of airbrush designed for modelers. Consult your hobby store owner or a fellow model club member with airbrush experience.

2. Go for a compressor to power your airbrush. The investment will be amply repaid.

3. Practice, practice. Consult other modelers and read book and journal features by airbrush experts. Learn how to control the airbrush until precision and accuracy become second nature to you.

4. Choose the type of paint that suits you best and stick to it. Avoid mixing different types of paint where possible.

5. Keep safe. Wear a disposable safety mask when spraying and never spray enamels or cellulose-base colors near a naked flame.

6. Last but by no means least, look after your equipment. Treat airbrushes with respect. They are delicate, precision instruments and if properly cared for will last a modeling lifetime. Clean airbrushes immediately after use and do it carefully, following the manufacturer's instructions. Keeping airbrush equipment

model to create roughly circular, random blotches. Such was the technique I used to finish the *Maiasaura* and the allosaurs on the cover. This method is extremely effective, and if you use up to three contrasting colors (cleaning the airbrush between each successive application), some exciting finishes can be achieved. Once you gain experience, more elaborate paint schemes of your own devising become possible. But for starters, keep it simple.

Continued on page 65

DINOGALLERY

Ceratosaurus, Jurassic, 150 MYA (million years ago). This is a Monsters in Motion resin kit. It comes from an original master by Tom Dickens. It is built as supplied with modifications, such as refining the teeth and adding internal nostrils, trachea, and cloaca—all from Milliput. In addition, the left foot position was drastically altered and remodeled to provide a more dramatic pose. Skin texture is superbly done and proves an ideal candidate for thinned tonal washes. At 17″ long, the model is about 1/12 scale.

Dilophosaurus, Jurassic, 200 MYA. Horizon's large scale *JP* "Spitter" was rebuilt with Milliput to lengthen its snout and remove evidence of the *JP* frill. New crests were added, a fourth finger to each hand, and the hollow body was stuffed with waste paper to alleviate its starved look. The hollow legs were filled with plaster and the jaws closed. For full authenticity, several upper jaw teeth should be visible. Hand painted and drybrushed, glass eyes finish the model. 1/10 scale.

Carnotaurus, Cretaceous, 97 MYA. A Lunar resin, this had cosmetic changes made to feet and claws as well as the usual internal jaw additions. The model is posed on a modified Lunar base that incorporates a *Parasaurolophus* carcass, here modified to represent a nonspecific hadrosaur. This base is sold with Lunar's *T. Rex–Velociraptor* set, the *Carnotaurus* paired with a *Hypacrosaurus.* It's very easy to mix and match when models are marketed to a constant scale, in this case 1/35. Original sculpture: Bob Morales.

Velociraptor, Cretaceous, 70 MYA. This little Kaiyodo resin is a simple repaint of a ready-painted display model in the Japanese manufacturer's Dinoland series. The model is integrally cast into a base, which was glued to a piece of sawed wood and blended in with modeling clay. The addition of pebbles and a stone completed the model, along with its new airbrushed paint scheme. 1/14 scale.

Tyrannosaurus Rex, Cretaceous, 68–65 MYA. This is the favorite of dinosaur kit manufacturers. Tamiya's is one of the best available and looks great in this speedy running pose. The kit's diorama parts were modified and integrated in one of the author's preferred wood bases. Real asparagus fern lacquered and sprayed green adds a further touch of vegetation alongside the kit's two cycad trees.

Troodon, Cretaceous, 73–65 MYA. Also known as *Stenonychosaurus, Troodon* is believed by scientists to have been one of the most intelligent of dinosaurs. This is an Invicta Plastics model, unique in their product line because of its larger scale and separate snap-on base. The one-piece plastic model has all seam lines removed and eye sockets drilled out for replacements. It is glued to a wood base. It was primed in acrylic white and painted entirely by stippling with a stiff nylon brush, starting with pale yellow for the belly, then lemon, light green, dark green, and finally black-green on the spine. 1/20 scale.

Baryonyx walkeri, Cretaceous, 120 MYA. The recent discovery in the United Kingdom of "heavy claw" caused a big stir in the paleoworld. This Saurian Studios resin does justice to the beast and is beautifully sculpted. Few modifications were required other than to clean up some seam lines and add glass eyes. The model was fully airbrushed over a matte white cellulose spray primer. 1/12 scale, original sculpture: Tom Dickens.

Apatosaurus (aka *Brontosaurus*), Jurassic, 156–150 MYA. One of the best known dinosaurs, this is an old Kaiyodo vinyl ready-assembled display model. On the author's example, the joined parts were poorly matched, with excess glue runs everywhere, a "starved" stomach, and splayed limbs. The model was pulled apart, the body stuffed, and the limbs repositioned before extensive filling was carried out. You can employ an airbrush finish over a cellulose primer coat. 1/35 scale.

Stegosaurus, Jurassic, 150 MYA. Another famous dinosaur that has been reinvented by scientists in the light of new discoveries. The exquisite vinyl version by Kaiyodo offers a more dynamic pose than earlier, more traditional models. Few modifications were necessary, other than moving the caudal spikes to horizontal positions and adding the armored dewlap to the throat. The finish is an airbrushed one, all the plates being treated separately. 1/20 scale.

Amargasaurus, Cretaceous, 131–125 MYA. This bizarre sauropod was recently discovered in Argentina and bears a series of paired elongated spines on neck, back, and tail vertebrae. This Kaiyodo resin kit features solid webbing between the spines, which calls out for liquid latex rubber replacement. (Spoiler alert: some scientists suggest there was no webbing between the spines. Your choice!) 1/35 scale.

Barosaurus, Jurassic, 150 MYA. One of Kaiyodo's most ambitious and largest resin dinosaur kits to date, this rare *Barosaurus* and juvenile were marketed with a prowling *Allosaurus* (see cover photo), together with a large base. The dramatic, full-size mount in New York's American Museum of Natural History inspired the set piece. In solid resin, the rearing female is weighty and demands care in handling. The fit of all leg parts was poor, and thus some remodeling was required. The juvenile's mouth was opened and a Milliput tongue added. Both models were firmly pinned to the wood base with wire leg inserts. 1/35 scale.

Edmontonia, Cretaceous, **74–72 MYA.** Yet another Lunar resin, this one paired with a *T. Rex* (not shown). Another simple model of few parts and thus easy to build, once all the mold seams are eradicated. The various spines will need refinement. You'll find the miniature *Edmontonia* to be just as prickly a customer as its full-sized counterpart undoubtedly was! Mind those fingers! **1/35 scale, original sculpture: Bob Morales.**

Anklyosaurus, Cretaceous, 70–65 MYA. This solid-looking beast is from a Kaiyodo vinyl, and as befits its subject, the kit parts are heavy and require plenty of heat softening when fitted together. The detailed skin and armor texture are enhanced by drybrushing various colors over an overall spray primer of matte black cellulose. 1/20 scale.

Maisaura, Cretaceous, 80–75 MYA. Stop thief! The peaceful *Maisaura* vainly guards her nest as a young *Dromiceiomimus* runs off with one of her eggs. Nest, egg thief, and eggs were all made up from scratch using Milliput, while real miniature fern leaves add a touch of detail to the base groundwork. 1/35 scale.

Parasaurolophus, Cretaceous, 68–65 MYA. The crested *Parasaurolophus* is another plastic kit from Tamiya and has been modified to give a more lively pose. A web has been added to the head crest with a very thin poly card suitably scribed. You could also make this from latex rubber. The paint scheme was based on a book illustration by John Sibbick, a well-known British paleoartist. The cycad tree is from the kit, as are some of the bones and rocks. Others are simply Milliput carefully painted to match the real stone. 1/35 scale.

Protoceratops, Cretaceous, 87–78 MYA. This is a fine one-piece resin casting from Saurian Studios, which requires only some cleaning up of seam lines. Glass eyes and a drybrushed, not sprayed, finish add realism. The beak and bony frill detail are accentuated by thin, dark brown washes over a matte ivory base. 1/5 scale, original sculpture: Michael Jones.

Kaiyodo's 1991 soft vinyl *Chasmosaurus* is beautifully molded with well-fitting parts. The model has had its head repositioned and resulting gaps filled with Milliput. The complex color scheme is a combination of airbrushing and hand painting. 1/20 scale, original sculpture: Shinobu Matsumura.

Dimetrodon, Permian-Triassic, 286–210 MYA. Popular with kit manufacturers, the pelycosaur *Dimetrodon* was not a dinosaur, but it's a great project for modelers. This Lunar resin kit features a scratch-built latex sail replacing the solid kit item, as described in chapter 6. 1/8 scale (approx.), original sculpture: Bob Morales.

Kronosaurus, Cretaceous, 127–108 MYA. Marine reptiles contemporary with the dinosaurs are becoming popular with kit manufacturers. Lunar Models' *Kronosaurus* contains but two body parts, making it an ideal first model. Here it sails over the seabed, courtesy of a wire mount camouflaged by rocks. Potpourri bags often yield colorful starfish. Ideal dressing for your diorama! 1/40 scale (approx.).

Tropeognathus robustus, Cretaceous, 119–113 MYA. This is one of a trio of resin pterosaurs released by Kaiyodo in 1995 (the others are *Pteranodon sternbergi* and *Quetzalcoatlus northropi*), incorporated here in a diorama. The pterosaur has had its wings replaced with tissue paper coated in liquid latex rubber. 1/32 scale (approx.).

For armored dinosaurs such as Lunar Models' *Edmontonia,* fully paint the belly and back and drybrush before painting the spikes, dorsal plates, and scutes. Then paint these ivory, followed by a thin wash of raw umber to define the detail. Next, apply a coat of matte clear varnish (which can dry slightly shiny) and drybrush the spike tips with matte white. This technique also works well on claws and the horns of ceratopsians, such as *Triceratops.*

This *Carnotaurus* is getting the dark wash treatment over its matte ivory horns and dorsal plates. Mix up matte clear varnish and raw umber to overpaint these small detail areas. The color will fill the molded detail and tinge it darker, thus adding depth. Run round the base of the horns and claws in the same way. Take your time.

Continued from page 48

absolutely clean is vital and something you should not skimp on, for if you neglect the airbrush, its performance will be seriously impaired.

Okay, lecture over. Now we can return to our dinosaurs and take a look at a few specific painting techniques.

HORNS AND CLAWS

Some of the most impressive features on dinosaurs are the horns of *Triceratops,* the tail spikes of *Stegosaurus,* and *Velociraptors'* sickle claws. I usually paint these in an ivory color, with a wash of dark brown concentrated on their bases and brushed toward the tips, which later are drybrushed off-white. Then I apply clear satin varnish overall. Claws can also be painted a dark gray, highlighted at their tips with a pale version of the same color. It's all down to personal preference.

JAWS

If you are modeling one of the large predatory theropods, the mouth will be a focal point. I usually spray the inside of the mouth with a mixture of beige, white, and pink to achieve a light salmon pink shade, later air- or drybrushed with pale pink. Tongues are a

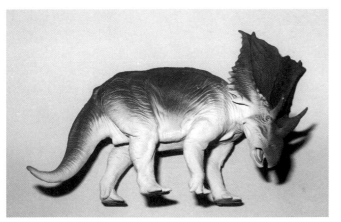

Coloring *Chasmosaurus.* This Kaiyodo vinyl has received a sprayed cellulose primer coat followed by an overall dark green wash. The lower areas are next sprayed in a pale cream color, as seen here.

Next spray a fawn beige color on the mid-section. Set your airbrush to fine and shade the flanks, leaving the lower color intact, bringing the new color half way up the sides.

Now for a pale lime, yellow green mix. Spray this higher up, leaving the mid band of ocher intact as shown. Spray along the sides and rear of the neck frill.

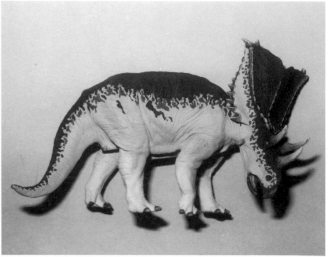

The upper dark green areas are handpainted over the yellow green areas, as shown. Medium green patches were then added beneath the darker color with a fine brush. All the horns and frill spikes have been painted ivory, followed by an umber-tinted varnish wash. Their tips were drybrushed off-white. Claws and beak are dark gray, drybrushed in light gray to highlight detail. The pink mouth area is coated with a mixture of satin clear varnish and a small amount of red water color. As a final touch, I drybrush most of my models with a matte or satin polyurethane varnish in one or two quick passes only. Don't coat the entire model. Merely catching some areas to give a slight sheen looks extremely realistic. Use restraint!

purplish blue-pink. Teeth are rarely pure white. Use an ivory color for teeth, then wash with a thin mix of yellow-brown. Look at your dog's teeth and you'll get the idea.

To finish, apply an overall coat of satin varnish tinted with a small amount of red paint. This mix can also be applied to accentuate the jaw adductor muscle. This is the web of skin bridging the back of the jaws just behind the teeth. It is more obvious on theropod models with open mouths, such as Tamiya's *T. Rex* and Kaiyodo's *Allosaurus* (see the photos). You can improve things even further by adding slight traces of red around your model's jaws, if it is a carnivore, or pale green to simulate chewed vegetation if it is a plant eater. Nostrils and ear slits can be picked out in dark red. All these areas can be emphasized with clear satin varnish once the paint has dried.

If your finished model is destined for a diorama base, don't forget to drybrush (or airbrush) the feet and belly to match the ground color you've decided upon. This can be done before or after the dinosaur's feet have been firmly planted in place.

PAINTING EYES

It is not always practical to use glass eyes on small scale dinosaurs, and so we will need to hand paint them. This will require time, patience, and a steady hand. I would also strongly recommend adding a bench-mounted magnifying glass.

Start by painting the entire eye socket (cornea) with off-white or ivory. When dry, this is given a thin wash of deep red to tint it. With a very fine, pointed brush outline the eye with deep pink and let dry. No one really knows what precise color or shape dinosaur

eyes were, so the round (or slit-shaped) iris can be any color you like: pale blue, vivid green, deep orange, or chrome yellow. You'll find it much easier to apply a really neat, circular iris if you cut the tip from a wooden toothpick, dip it into the paint, and dot the eye. Here's where that stand-mounted magnifier comes in handy. The darker pupil is a simple, smaller black dot in the center of the iris. The sharp, uncut point of a toothpick may be employed to apply it; or you could use a fine-nibbed, say 0.10, drafter's pen filled with black ink.

Once the eyes have been painted to your satisfaction, brush the entire cornea with a thick coat of Kristal Klear. Build it up to provide a bulged appearance. Allow to dry.

Eyelids are fairly easy to reproduce. On larger models with glass eyes, you can use small skeins of filler suitably shaped and scored to represent wrinkles. Mask the eyes first with PVA white glue and apply the filler. Shape as required—you'll need care here—and leave to harden. When they are dry, paint the lids to match the surrounding skin color, then carefully score around the eye with a sharp knife and pick off the dried PVA skin. On smaller models, eyelids can be simulated by thick applications of paint; for closed eyes, simply fill the molded cornea. To finish off Kristal Klear

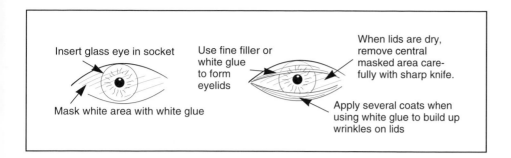

Insert glass eye in socket

Use fine filler or white glue to form eyelids

When lids are dry, remove central masked area carefully with sharp knife.

Mask white area with white glue

Apply several coats when using white glue to build up wrinkles on lids

eyes, just apply transparent gloss varnish to seal them and add a little sparkle.

Before leaving the topic of painting, a word or two about varnishing. Several brands of clear varnish are available for model work, but treat them with caution. Never use pure gloss varnish as a finish other than for glazing eyes, adding saliva, or creating water effects. For an overall, final finish I drybrush matte varnish over the model, which further emphasizes the skin texture and imparts a realistic patina to the surface.

As mentioned previously, I tend to employ satin varnish to finish off mouth interiors, since standard gloss is too powerful for small scale models and appears artificial and toylike. You can control the degree of a satin, semimatte (or semigloss, if you prefer) finish by mixing together matte and gloss varnishes to suit your particular requirements.

Art stores will also provide a selection of matte aerosol sprays for fixing, and some of these can be employed to cover large models and diorama bases. But do experiment *first*. Not all model paints take kindly to these types of spray, so test them out on scrap pieces of painted material before spraying your model. And please wear a face mask!

5

YOUR OWN "LOST WORLD"

Many modelers of my acquaintance care little about dioramas, being content to display their masterpieces in a cabinet or on book shelves. That's okay. You can display your model dinosaurs in exactly the same way, especially if space is at a premium. I feel, though, that if you are portraying a living animal (even an extinct one), it will look so much more realistic posed on a carefully composed organic, scenic base.

There are many proficient exponents of the diorama art around who have written some wonderful articles and books on the subject. Consult the relevant references cited in the appendixes. I recommend anything written by Shep Paine.

We'll start here with a simple base before working up to more involved versions and full dioramas.

FIRST BASE

A number of commercial outlets offer custom-made display bases, plinths, and cases, etc., which are all ideal. You can also create some of these for yourself.

In the same way that I prefer natural, informal garden pools to formal, square ones, my preference is for natural wood bases: sliced-through 1″ deep sections of trunks or branches. Some woodworkers and wood turners may provide these, or timber merchants can cut them for you.

Hardwoods such as burr oak or burr elm are good for this purpose. They can be drilled to hold wire leg supports, and the natural grain and growth rings can be incorporated into the terrain later. Some sections will have large knot holes of irregular shape. These can be filled with clear polyester resin or faced with rippled

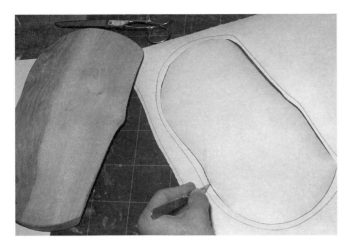 

Whatever type of base you select, the underside should be faced with felt or a similar material to protect those surfaces on which the completed model is to be placed. This is easy. You can obtain self-adhesive felt material from hardware stores. Just place the base on top, trace round the outline with a pencil, then cut the material about half an inch from the marked outline.

Remove the felt from the backing paper, reverse the base, and simply press down to secure it. Job done!

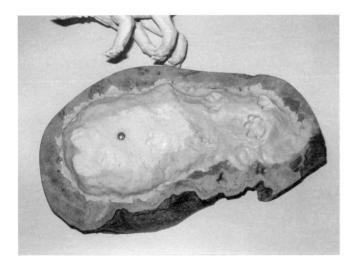

Some resin kits include bases of their own, and you may wish to use them. In the case of Saurian Studios' *Protoceratops*, the resin base was screwed to a wooden one and super glued around the edges. DasPronto modeling clay was built up around and over the casting. Shape it with your fingers, using water to make the clay easier to use. This is especially helpful when pressing the model's feet into the clay to leave footprints. Don't forget to cover up that screw head!

Now paint the top of the base in a matte dark earth and position your model as you choose. If it's a simple, four-legged creature, it won't require support pegs. Scrape away any paint from the soles of the feet and the corresponding areas of the base. Super glue to secure it.

Once it is dry, apply PVA white wood glue all over the base with an old brush. Work it around the feet and between the toes and claws if present. Now dress the base with grit. You can obtain commercially available ground texture materials from hobby shops, but these are usually too uniform and thus somewhat unrealistic. You really need a natural selection of various sizes. The solution is in your own backyard or sidewalk. Here you will find unlimited amounts of miniature sand, rocks, and pebbles. Just dust them up into a jar and sprinkle over the still wet PVA glue. Allow to set and then blow the excess grit away. You can either leave it untreated or else paint and drybrush overall for different color soil effects.

Variations on the same theme include the addition of rocks or trees, vegetation, and other, smaller contemporary creatures. First, though, we need to look at building up the ground area for greater realism.

SECOND BASE

Several resin dinosaur manufacturers provide bases with their kits, pretextured and often incorporating rocks, plants, etc., into the casting. All you need do is paint them and glue your model in place. Done!

You may also wish to marry the kit base with your own wooden one. Simple! Merely drill a few holes through the resin and with wood screws, fix the two firmly together. Run super glue all around the base to anchor it securely, and leave to set.

Resin bases can be blended into wooden ones by adding modeling clay around the edges, smoothing it

clear plastic "water" to produce ponds or drinking holes. But use square bases if you prefer.

Whatever type you select, it's a good idea to face the undersurface with a self-adhesive "flock" material to protect the surface the finished model is to stand on. You can obtain self-adhesive green or red felt material from hardware stores.

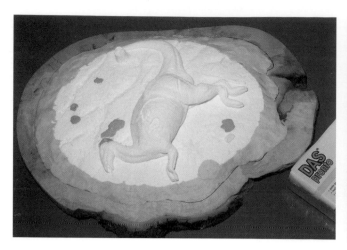

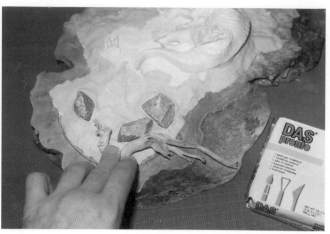

Here's the same technique on another resin base. This is from a Lunar Models' kit. Three screws have been used to firmly secure the resin to the wood before being covered with filler. DasPronto blends the edges into the wood surface. As the clay dries out, it will shrink and leave a gap all around the feathered edges. Use PVA wood glue to fill and fix it.

This diorama base is enhanced by embedding small stones (rocks) and driftwood into the DasPronto groundwork. When, dry these extras can be lifted out, painted as desired, and later glued into position.

to feather the material outwards. Wet your fingers and sculpt. I use DasPronto for diorama work. Available in white or terra-cotta, it is air-drying, easy to work, dries fairly quickly, and is reasonably inexpensive. Some modelers use Super Sculpey, but remember this needs to be hardened by baking, so the wood will have to go into the oven as well. Be careful if you adopt this approach. Softwoods will split when heated, but hard ones such as ash should be okay.

Milliput can be used for groundwork, but is best for smaller areas or where bonding is required. Using it over really large areas would prove rather expen-

sive; DasPronto is far more economical. While this modeling clay sets, you can use its slow drying time to your advantage.

Rocks can be embedded into DasPronto while it dries, as can driftwood trees and stumps. You can also make dinosaur footprints by simply pressing your model's feet along the base before temporarily planting it in its intended final position. When the clay is semidry, remove these items and clean off any residual material.

As DasPronto dries, it tends to shrink, and you may need to make good later when refitting your

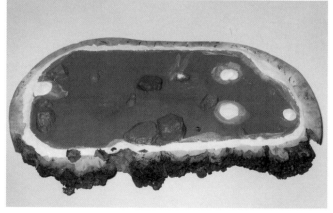

Tamiya dinosaurs come with complete sets of parts for diorama bases. These parts can be modified for incorporation into your own display. Saw off the raised sides of the kit base and screw it to your wood base, as shown. For drilling pilot holes, choose the depressions intended for the kit's rocks. Later you can use these to cover up the screw heads. Simple!

Here's the Tamiya *T. Rex* base shown previously. The edges have been sealed with Milliput and blended to the wood surface. Most of the screw heads have been hidden by filler and rocks.

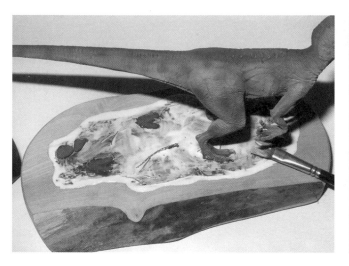

Your dried base can now be given an undercoat of matte enamel paint—Humbrol dark earth, in this case. Now coat the surface with PVA white wood glue applied liberally by brush. The model can either be glued in place first or left until later. It's your choice.

Sprinkle a mixture of road grit, fine grain sand, scenic material—or a combination of all three—over the wet PVA glue. Leave for ten minutes then shake the model over a large sheet of scrap paper. Save the unglued droppings for another model.

scenic pieces and finished model and gluing them in place. PVA wood glue can be used as a combined filler-adhesive before dressing the base overall with grit material.

You can use natural small rocks gathered from outdoors for your diorama. Do select only those that are rough edged, not eroded, round ones, which will look unnatural. Rocks must be firmly embedded into the modeling clay and not just sit on top of the ground. Natural rocks can be left in their original colors, or you can paint and drybrush them to suit.

Suitable trees, whether modeled as living organisms or dead, petrified trunks, can be adapted from driftwood. Walking the seashore is recommended for diorama modelers. You can use dry seaweed, small shells, old dead tree branches and twigs, and volcanic sand to great effect. If using natural driftwood, however, you may want to have it fumigated to remove any insect larvae that might still be present.

Those of you who have already built some of Tamiya's dinosaur kits will have had the benefit of fully integrated diorama pieces already included. Typically thorough, Tamiya provides trees, rocks, and dinosaur skulls and bones, as well as contemporary pterosaurs, lizards, frogs, and fish, where appropriate. The bases on four of the kits are designed to match up and make one big display—neat. But you can adapt the kit bases by sawing off all four sides and screwing the molded top surface to a wood plinth, adding Milliput around the edges so that the plastic terrain is blended into the new base. Disguise any gaps or ridges with grit applied over PVA wood glue, then paint as desired. The photos will clarify the techniques.

Vegetation: Expert modelers like Shep Paine have come up with some great ideas to represent vegetation and trees for dioramas. Some of these sound techniques can be adopted for dinosaur models with a few caveats. First, there's static grass, available commercially in hobby stores. This is applied just like grit or sand: brush white glue over the desired areas, sprinkle on generous amounts of static grass and blow away the excess. When dried, it can be painted deep green and drybrushed yellow to simulate moss. Moss, but not grass. Why? Because there were no grasses around when dinosaurs ruled the Earth, so they have no place in any authentic diorama. Low-growing vegetation, like trees, is notoriously difficult to model convincingly, and often a representation of foliage looks far more realistic in small scales than a leaf-by-leaf, twig-by-twig reconstruction.

Once again, natural materials are recommended. Small bushes can be made out of dried flowers, or try small leaves and twigs from a potpourri bag. Visiting a florist's store will yield a wide choice of such material and other items you can adapt. Dried, everlasting flowers often produce dozens of tiny heads that can be dyed in any shade you wish using thinned-down water colors. Be aware that flowering plants, such as magnolias, did not appear until the Cretaceous period. So no flowers in Jurassic Park, please!

Railroad modelers often make use of dried lichen, which is available commercially in usually very bright greens. I would apply this material sparingly and at the very least wash it and restain with thinned, brown fabric dye to deaden the original color. Lichen is also better when broken apart to form irregular shapes that will look far more natural.

Here a small Kaiyodo *Dilophosaurus* has been secured to a section of wood sliced from a small tree branch. No clay was used, just matte paint covered in PVA, then an application of fine volcanic sand. You can leave unglued patches to give a more irregular terrain. After painting, and after firmly fixing the sand, you can use drybrushing techniques to enhance the textured groundwork.

What about adding partial skeletons, as well as stones and driftwood, to the scenic base? Tamiya provides skulls and bones with some of their kits, but you can also use a complete set of remains. Here most of a Glencoe *Stegosaurus* kit is embedded in Polyfilla to enhance the display of a Kaiyodo *Allosaurus*.

Miniature tree trunks and branches are not just available from the shoreline; a trip to the local forest will yield plenty of material. Search out young shoots and small roots; the latter make particularly good miniature trees. Choose and dig out several different kinds and sizes and rinse them with water before drying out thoroughly before use. Remember that natural materials work best, and that's true of trees, although

this is not always practical. As mentioned earlier, reproduction of foliage is never easy and demands both time and patience.

I've made use of garden moss for some groundwork, and the stringy variety (available in florists for use in hanging baskets) can be employed for some types of tree. Try dried seaweed for creepers and other foliage effects. Of course, it's not essential to create an

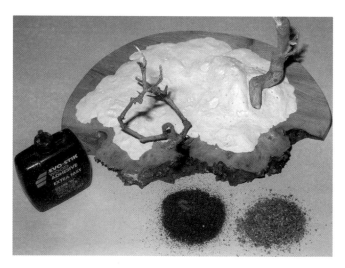

This is the start of a scene involving a tussle between two *Pachyrhinosaurus* male rivals. DasPronto was applied to the base, and two pieces of driftwood embedded after the models were test-fitted to the still-wet base. Use the models to make footprints and punch holes all over the base with a toothpick. Not only does this speed drying of the clay, but afterward you can plant flowers and fungi in the holes. Sand and forest litter await application.

Static grass, used by military and railroad modelers, is great for moss on trees and rocks. Brush on PVA white glue, then add the grass. Moss should appear on only one side of the diorama only.

Some commercially available scenic materials can supplement those freely available outdoors. Hudson and Allen Studio, for example, provide military modelers with a wide range of goodies. Here their "forest litter" is being applied to the painted base over PVA glue and pregritted areas.

Remember all those holes we made? You can use dried flowers cut up into individual pieces and planted with PVA glue to secure them. Florists sell large varieties of pot-pourri and dried flowers that can be used for diorama work. Those shown are taken from *Limonium fruticans,* native to the Canary Islands.

entire forest for your diorama; a dead stump or rotted, fallen trunk is often all that's required. You have to decide what you wish to convey in the set piece.

Ferns and conifer trees were abundant during the reign of the dinosaurs, but for modelers, these prove the most difficult of trees to reproduce in miniature. Real mosses and ferns, particular the delicate asparagus fern, make ideal foliage for some evergreens; and for large conifers and redwoods, you need to make up the trunks yourself. Some scenic material manufacturers market kits for tropical palms, and these usually

employ white metal for trunks and etched brass for the branches and leaves. They can look extremely convincing, but don't expect to finish them in an evening. Shep Paine creates realistic pine tree trunks from wooden dowels carefully carved to shape, drilling them at regular intervals for insertion of branches. Bark detail can be simulated by modeling putty or Milliput and carefully studying real trees for the correct form your sculpting should take.

It's well worth taking a notebook and camera on your field trips to gather natural materials. Observe

Tamiya's *T. Rex* base has been completely incorporated into a larger wood plinth. Aside from the extra filler and rocks, further dressing has been added using kit parts, sidewalk grit and stones, and real miniature foliage (asparagus fern) fixed with artist's spraymount. Finish overall with a matte clear spray.

Tamiya provides cycads with its *T. Rex* kit. The trunks are plastic, the fronds cut from green crepe paper stiffened by coated wire stems. The idea works well, but assembly requires patience. You'll find that stripping the wire covering will aid adhesion to the paper leaves.

Typical modern palm trees. True small scale reproduction is not easy, although etched-brass accessory kits available commercially do make life easier for the diorama modeler. Thin paper seems to be the best material to make feathery stems and leaves.

Making authentic-looking palm trees and cycads is not easy, as anyone who studies them will readily testify. This is a modern Chinese fan palm, similar to some ancient trees, which gives you an idea of what's involved. Prehistoric plants that have survived to this day include conifers, magnolias, horsetails, and ginkgoes.

nature in all seasons and weather conditions. Half an hour walking the dog will give you plenty of ideas and fire your imagination. Study palm trees, conifers, and ferns before trying to model them. Pay particular attention to colors.

Cycads: Cycads were the dominant order of plants in the Mesozoic era. Cycads had palmlike crowns from which stems of fernlike leaves grew. They formed an important part of the diet for many plant-eating dinosaurs. These plants flourished from the Triassic right through to the Cretaceous, but only one species appears to exist today, *Cycas revoluta,* the Japanese sago palm, which can also be found in Bonsai displays. The latter may also prove very useful for model dinosaur displays.

Tamiya provides some well-designed cycads in their *T. Rex* and *Parasaurolophus* kits, which are quite

realistic. Other cycad trunks can be replicated from real conifer or pine cones, coated with super glue to seal them before painting and finally drybrushed to highlight detail. Drill out the crown (top) to more easily insert etched-brass fern leaves sprayed matte yellow-green; you can also use pieces of real asparagus fern for the same purpose. The fir cones may be randomly drilled to accept small, dried flower heads, if desired. When adding these, keep them odd-numbered—three, seven, nine etc. This is an old diorama trick. Many modelers will recommend three rocks as more natural than four; three or five trees more realistic than six or eight. Adopt and adapt their ideas. Experiment. Enjoy!

Water: We'll be looking at seascapes in the next chapter, but you may wish to consider some water or swamp effects for dinosaur dioramas. Small pools or drinking holes will form interesting focal points for your models.

Once again we may turn to our model railroader colleagues for one solution—molded water. Sheets of clear, rippled plastic are available and supplied with a pale blue paper undersheet for river and lake effects. I've found the plastic, if it is thumbtacked securely over a prepared base, ideal for suggesting surface water. This can either be a deep depression painted and dressed with small stones, weed, and miniature fish, or merely a precolored flat base. Both types are illustrated here. The trick is to ensure that the sheet remains perfectly flat when fixed, and plenty of tacks

Semi-scratchbuilt cycads

Brush on white glue or varnish to seal

Drill out holes; insert etched fronds in top, flower heads around trunk will be required. Use two-pack epoxy glues for really firm surface bonding. Milliput rocks and plants may be situated to disguise the heads of the thumbtacks before dressing.

More involved set pieces can involve the use of clear polyester resin available in craft stores for embedding purposes. It can be tinted in any color you choose, and being transparent will provide a realistic impression of depth. Be warned, however: Resin vapors are extremely toxic and should never be mixed and used other than in a fully ventilated area. Always wear a face mask. Resin hardens by a catalytic reaction that tends to generate a great deal of heat, which will readily melt plastic and vinyl models as well as affecting certain types of paint. Water-base colors appear to be immune, but you would be well advised to test any polyester resin on various pieces of scrap material before risking your precious model. I hardly ever make use of clear resins; their fumes give me severe sinus problems. But that's just my personal choice. You may, of course, find resin ideal for dioramas and take to it like a "duckbill to water." If so, then a whole new world will open up, and some spectacular models may result.

THIRD BASE

With several of my dinosaur dioramas, I've tried to tell a story, showing aspects of dinosaur lifestyles and providing the basic models with a little more realism. The sleepy *Allosaurus* in a forest glade was my first attempt at such a diorama, and while by no means perfect, the result was reasonably successful enough to encourage me to try a few more.

The box used for the diorama was an old stereo hi-fi speaker cabinet with its contents stripped out and the mesh removed. My local picture framer made up a matching glass door for the open front, which I added at the final stage, with small brass hinges and securing catches. Of course, if you are adept at woodworking, you can make your own boxes.

The next step was to secure a curved section of plywood or hardwood to the rear and front edges of the box to form a panoramic backdrop. This doesn't have to be a perfect fit, since the scenery and groundwork will later disguise any gaps.

One of my usual natural wood bases was then screwed and glued to the floor of the box and a piece of driftwood added. The whole lot was blended together with liberal applications of terra-cotta DasPronto. As the clay slowly dries, press your semifinished dinosaur model firmly into the clay to form a realistic depression; remove the model and wash away any residual clay.

To speed up the drying of the layered, thickly applied DasPronto, make lots of deep holes with a toothpick all over the ground area. These holes will also prove useful later on for planting flowers, stalks, and fungi, among other things. Those holes that will not be so employed may be filled or covered with surface texture detail.

Now select a suitable scenic background for your box. You can paint this yourself on thin art board, use a blown-up photo image, or, as in my case, glue part of a commercially available print in place. This print was taken, appropriately enough, from Matt Kalmenoff's

Stop, thief! It's not all that difficult to make a dinosaur nest from modeling clay. You can create it when making up the base terrain by forming a simple crater, rolling the clay between thumb and forefinger. The eggs are made from Milliput, as is the egg-stealing dromaeosaurid.

This base is completely dressed with volcanic sand, forest litter, rocks, and grit. Not visible here are the large number of small holes drilled at irregular intervals all around the base.

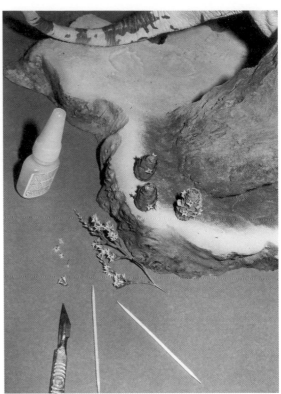

Fir tree sprigs and pieces of asparagus fern have been sprayed in hair lacquer to fix them before airbrushing in green tones. They need not be fixed permanently; just push them into the predrilled holes once the model dinosaur has been fixed in place.

Real fir cones can be used to simulate cycad trunks. Varnish, or coat with super glue, then drill the top to accept leaves later. Here dried flowers are cut up and individual heads glued around the trunk, in odd numbers only—five, seven, nine, etc.

Dinosaur Dioramas, a book of cut-out-and-assemble card dinosaurs and backgrounds.

Plan your box diorama with care. Sketch out some designs and make notes at an early stage. I had wanted to place my converted Kaiyodo vinyl *Allosaurus* in a forest clearing, but obviously, incorporating complete conifers or giant redwoods would have been impractical. Thus, only the bases of tree trunks were reproduced, cut from some dead pine branches, and drilled at random for adding small twigs and foliage. The roof of the box is similarly drilled and then painted in mottled greens to simulate a forest canopy. This won't be immediately obvious when viewing the model, and once hanging twigs and branches are glued to the roof, an impression of a forest will be achieved. The real twigs were dressed with pine boughs marketed by Hudson and Allen Studios, whose equally excellent "forest litter" dressed the forest clearing after painting.

Etched-brass accessory kits provide fern leaves and palm trees. These can make convincing replicas, but will prove expensive if you want to use a lot of them. They are also quite time-consuming to assemble.

Etched-brass fern leaves have been airbrushed (do this in an old shoe box so the leaves won't escape!). They are later glued to the cycad trunks with PVA wood glue.

This elaborate section of wood has a large section missing, making an ideal pool. First the bottom is dressed with grit and stones. Paint fully before adding aquatic plants (dried seaweed), fish, and salamanders for further realism.

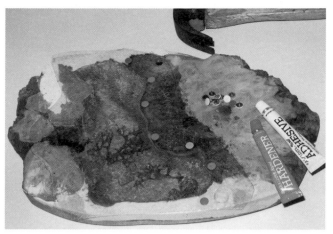

Now pin a section of rippled, clear plastic water (as used by model railroaders). Glue with two-part epoxy adhesive and keep it flat, using plenty of thumbtacks. Later all excess material can be covered with filler, modeling clay, grit, and more stones. It takes time, but the result is well worth the effort.

You can detail and paint the base of the diorama by using many of the techniques already described. Keep ground colors toned down, making background colors lighter than foreground ones. Static grass was applied to the outward-facing sides of the tree trunks and ground areas, with dyed lichen bushes added behind the rear trees to provide depth and blend the scene into the rear background painting. The drying holes may now be used to plant Milliput fungi, or they can be covered up with surface dressing before adding the background cycad.

The *Allosaurus* itself was a 1/35 scale Kaiyodo vinyl. Its dramatic molded pose was altered by cementing the jaws together and filling the resultant gap with Milliput. The forelimbs were glued in different positions and the left hand leg separated in three pieces. The right leg would not have been visible on completion, so I relegated it to the spares box. The modified left leg was glued in the position shown and gaps carefully filled. Those gaps left under the legs will be hidden once the model is pressed into its diorama base. You may need to modify the *Allosaurus*'s position to suit

When gluing, blend the feet into the terrain. The impressions of the model's feet should already have been formed before painting. Use two-part epoxy resin with steel rod or wire pegs to hold the model firmly. Here any gaps are being filled with white wood glue. Blow dust or fine powder or grit to the glue before it dries, then with an airbrush dust the feet and legs for a final touch.

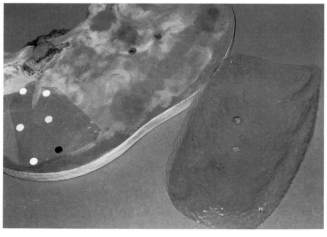

Here is a variation on the rippled water technique. First the plain base is painted deep ocher; then sections of the plastic are pinned in place. The reverse of the largest piece is painted blood red first. Why? Read on.

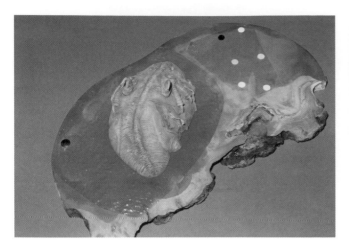

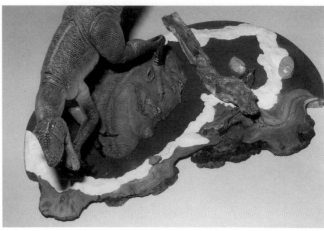

Pin the blood-stained water paint side down, to the wood base. Now attach the prepainted carcass; this was secured by screwing up into the resin molding from beneath the base. Countersink the wood to let in the screw heads before adding the underfelt. Run Kristal Klear all around the base of the resin body to anchor it to the plastic and also serve as a filler. Mix with some red water color first.

Next, build up the water's edge with Milliput, then DasPronto, to form a bank. Dress with grit and stones as before. The semicomplete Vector *Utahraptor* is then mounted on the blood-drenched back of its partially submerged victim.

the scene; I thought it looked natural to have its head resting on the fallen tree trunk.

Once completely painted, the *Allosaurus* was glued to its predetermined position with super glue. Any final gaps around the model may be filled with PVA white glue, gritted over if required, and painted to match the surrounding terrain.

As a final touch, I raided Tamiya's Mesozoic Creatures set for a perching *Archaeopteryx*. A slight reshaping of its head converted the kit's Cretaceous *Hypsilophodon* to the more appropriate Jurassic *Dryosaurus*.

As your confidence and prowess grow, you will be able to create really exciting and dramatic dioramas. Use small scale models, such as those produced by Battat and Invicta, to populate the backgrounds of your models to achieve a realistic-looking enforced perspective. Combine constant scale models for greater effect. Groups of hadrosaurs at a water hole would look neat, or what about sauropods fording a stream? Packs of *Velociraptors* attacking a duckbill would make a dramatic scene as would egg-laying dinosaurs and their nests.

This Wieger *T. Rex* has been glued and pinned to its base before any ground dressing has been applied. Run PVA glue around the feet and toes and sprinkle on the grit; shake loose when dry. Then add pressed fern leaves, fixed down by PVA wood glue.

When the model is firmly secured to the base, dust its feet to match the ground. Pastels were used over the undersides, legs, and lower body of this Kaiyodo *Maisaura* to provide a pleasing, weathered appearance.

Building box dioramas: An old speaker box with a curved piece of thin wood glued in place to form a backdrop. After adding a wood base and tree section, I built up the ground area with layers of DasPronto and embedded a converted *Allosaurus* temporarily into the clay. Note the toothpick at right for making dozens of drying holes.

A commercial printed background has been glued to the backdrop. Real conifer tree branches, split down their centers, are fixed to the rear of the box, covering gaps in the undersize backdrop painting. Complete sections of branch can be used for the foreground tree trunks.

Test-fit the semicompleted model to the diorama. If the clay has shrunk—it will!—add some more to lessen the gaps around the dinosaur, which can now be removed for final painting. Note extra filler at right, blending the terrain into the background.

The ground can now be painted and dressed. Do this carefully, especially around the rear. Lighten the colors as you progress to the back of the box. Use static grass to provide moss on bank and tree trunks.

The roof won't be readily visible, so a pseudo-forest canopy is painted, then the wood is drilled to accept pine tree twigs, which will hang down toward the ground. These are then dressed with pine boughs available from Hudson and Allen Studio product lines.

The base is complete with forest litter groundwork and painted lichen to the rear. The cycad is built of etched-brass leaves and dried flowers glued to a natural fir cone. Masking tape keeps paint from the outer edges. Once the dinosaur has been added, a glass door completes the job.

With experience, your imagination will be the only limit, but please do consult reliable references when combining dinosaur types. Check out when and where they lived, and the form of plant life contemporary with the chosen subject. Even basic research can prevent some avoidable goofs.

6

THE NONDINOSAURS

Question: When is a dinosaur not a dinosaur? Answer: When it is a pelycosaur, plesiosaur, or pterosaur. Nevertheless, this hasn't stopped some writers or model manufacturers from lumping these together under generic dinosaur classifications. Recent years have witnessed the release of a growing number of nondinosaur models and kits. Since many subjects were contemporary with dinosaurs, this opens up some fascinating diorama possibilities. But first we have to step back in time, way back to the distant Permian and Triassic periods, many millions of years before the first dinosaurs evolved. In this early era, large mammal-like reptiles thrived, and one of the best known of these was the sail-backed *Dimetrodon,* a pelycosaur. This fearsome meat-eater is understandably popular and has been the subject of several plastic kits as well as a few resin ones in recent years.

The enormous sail of *Dimetrodon* is its most distinctive feature, and many scientists believe it was covered by a web of skin through which blood was

Setting sail. The original *Dimetrodon* resin sail molding is shown beneath the completed latex version, which has just been peeled from the kit part. Beyond is the foil impression that helps serve as a template for the new sail spines.

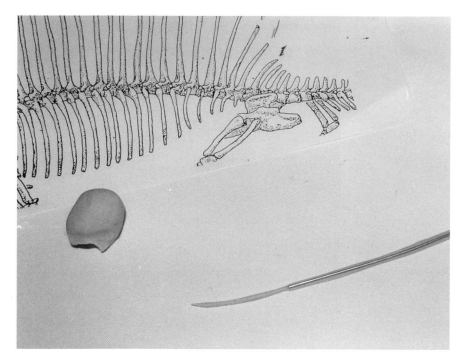

Rolling up spines from Super Sculpey. Note the xerox-enlarged reference drawing. Here one of the two wire internal supports is being wrapped with the polymer clay before being finally shaped, then baked.

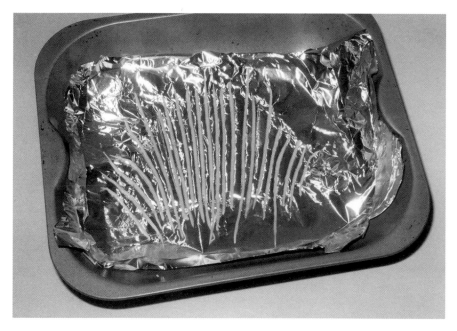

The completed spines are placed on the tin foil. Trim and shape the upper tips roughly to size using the kit part or foil impression as a template. Arrange the spines along the foil grooves to preserve their shape while baking.

pumped, acting as a kind of solar panel or radiator to control body temperature. It may also have served as a recognition feature or could even have changed color dur-ing mating seasons. We'll never know for certain. Whatever its real purpose, the sail was not solid and would have appeared translucent, an appearance well worth trying to emulate realistically in model form. Kit versions are unconvincing because of molding limitations. The sails are too thick in section, and even careful painting will not alter their solid look. I really wanted to achieve a semitransparent sail, and after several abortive attempts, I finally came up with a workable solution to the problem.

Having already produced a reasonably convincing web for Kaiyodo's *Parasaurolophus* by using liquid latex rubber, I merely adapted the process for *Dimetrodon*. The selected model was Lunar Models' resin kit, which I assembled after carefully cutting away the base of the sail molded integrally along the backbone. This area was then cleaned up with files and carbide paper. I did this before setting the model aside while the new sail was being prepared.

The Lunar kit's sail is a one-piece resin molding, which I carefully cleaned up before firmly pressing it to a large section of aluminum foil. You will need to trim the foil along the lower edge of the sail while ensuring that all the molded spines have made clearly defined impressions.

Now coat one side of the resin sail with liquid latex rubber and leave to dry. Apply up to three further coats of latex, allowing at least 12 hours' drying time between them. When the latex is fully cured, you can gently peel off what should be a rubbery, transparent version of the kit's original sail.

The next stage is a slightly more involved one: you need to fabricate new spines. There are 23 of these on Lunar's model, and I made them by rolling out various snakes of Super Sculpey. They don't have to be perfectly circular in section and will obviously be of varying lengths; few are completely straight. Using the aluminum foil as a guide, lay each of the spines along the corresponding impressed grooves, allowing at least an inch

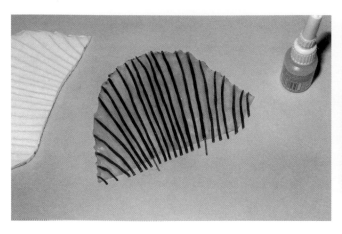

Once the baked spines have cooled, flip over the latex sail and fix all spines to their appropriate grooves with super glue. Ensure that the lower ends of all spines project beyond the lower edge of the sail.

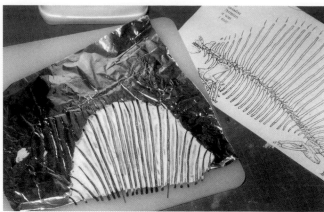

Place the latex sail, spines uppermost, on the foil so that the lower edge stands away from the work top. Now apply four or five coats of liquid latex over the spines and inner sail surface.

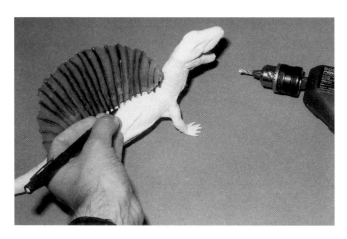

Your new sail will be semirigid and may be stretched slightly for fitting. Here the wire spines have been pushed into predrilled holes, while the others have their centers marked before further drilling ensues.

The sail has been trimmed, test-fitted, and finally glued. Now comes the time-consuming task of handpainting blood vessels and nerves on both sides. Once the paint has dried, apply another coat or two of latex and allow to dry before airbrushing the model in your desired colors. Now you're done!

of spine to project beyond the lower edge of the foil.

At least two of the spines will need to be rigid to impart some strength when you fit the sail later. You can roll some Super Sculpey around two lengths of carefully prebent piano wire. Chose equidistant spines for these wire supports; counting eight in from each end should suffice. Keeping the shapes in their tin foil grooves, bake the whole lot in the oven for about five minutes at slightly less than the polymer clay manufacturer's recommended temperature. It's easy to overcook small pieces of Super Sculpey, so do be careful.

Once baked and cooled, the spines will be quite fragile, so handle them gently. Flip over the latex sail and position the spines one at a time in each of the appropriate grooves. The shaped tips of the spines should protrude slightly from the top of the sail, but

their opposite ends must remain at least an inch beyond the lower edge. Spot glue the spines securely with Zap or similar cyano adhesive. Now position the sail onto the foil. It's important that you keep the lower edge of the sail above the surface of the work top to avoid excess latex sticking to it. Either roll up the foil to increase its thickness or place an old wooden ruler underneath the sail.

Next you'll need to apply four or more coats of latex rubber over the spines and to the inner surfaces of the first latex half. Leave it to dry fully. The result should be a semirigid sail with spines encased inside the layers of latex. It can be slightly stretched when fitting, but it is easily damaged, so don't be too heavy-handed. If required, trim the upper edges of the sail with a sharp knife, then use the lower projecting lengths of each spine to mark out corresponding drilling points along the model's backbone. Drill each hole ensuring that those for the two wire inserts are of smaller diameter to achieve a tight fit. Now test install the new sail, trimming the ends of the spines and opening up the holes as necessary. Finally, press the sail into place and run super glue along each side of the joint. Any gaps may be filled with PVA white glue. Restore the pebbly skin texture of the *Dimetrodon's* back (removed by earlier cutting and sanding) with blobs of white glue applied via a toothpick.

The latex sail can now be painted with red and purple matte enamels, using a fine brush to suggest blood vessels and nerves. When the paint has dried, brush one or two further coats of latex to both sides of the sail and seal in your delicate brushwork. Now airbrush lightly overall in your chosen color, or colors. But take care not to apply too many paint layers, otherwise the translucent membrane, with its delicate network of vessels, will be obscured, and you will have wasted all that careful work. Hold the model up to the light and check out the effect. Looks great, doesn't it?

Similar techniques can also be adopted for sail-backed dinosaurs, such as *Spinosaurus, Acrocanthosaurus, Ouranosaurus,* and *Armargasaurus,* and will really make them come alive.

SEA DRAGONS

The marine reptiles of the Mesozoic were fearsome creatures. Forget modern-day sharks, some of these extinct sea monsters would make Jaws look like whitebait. Model kits of giant mosasaurs and plesiosaurs are gaining popularity with manufacturers, making really impressive models that are comparatively simple to build. Kaiyodo's 1/20 scale vinyl *Elasmosaurus,* for example, has only five parts, while Lunar Models' *Kronosaur* has a mere two.

The techniques discussed in previous chapters are equally valid here, but there are a few special considerations for marine reptiles. The hollow body of Kaiyodo's *Elasmosaurus* was liberally stuffed with scrap newspaper, tin foil, and old plastic bags to give it more weight. After all, plesiosaurs were supposed to have swallowed stones for ballast! The four flippers fit reasonably well to the body recesses, but will still leave minor gaps to fill. Roll up very fine ribbons of Milliput and loop them round the entire circumference of the joints. Use plenty of water, pressing and smoothing the Milliput into place until the gaps are blended into the skin folds. Spray the entire model with matte white auto primer and check your work. Once satisfied, you can prime the model again; the white can remain as the underside color, while you spray or paint the darker upper surfaces. I chose deep blue grays with darker gray mottling over the top and sides. Look at pictures of sharks or dogfish to give you ideas for camouflage.

The display of your completed marine reptiles will require some careful thought. Unlike dinosaurs, plesiosaurs and mosasaurs tend to look awkward if left free-standing—like fish out of water! Some form of display mounting will therefore be more or less mandatory and can take similar forms to those already described. To give the illusion of free-swimming creatures, fix the models with wire supports, the shanks hidden by strategically placed rocks. Dress the base with appropriate marine life, such as dried starfish, seaweed, or shells. Spending a few hours beachcombing the shoreline should yield a profitable harvest.

Here is an underwater base for Lunar Models' *Kronosaurus* and its prey, a Kaiyodo ready-painted resin *Mosasaur.* The seabed is DasPronto wet-sculpted with the fingers. Strategically placed rocks surround vertical wire mounts that fit right up into the models' bellies.

Similar techniques were employed for Kaiyodo's 1/20 scale *Elasmosaurus,* but the selected rocks did not disguise the mounting rod entirely, hence the ball of Milliput to bridge the gap and complete the illusion. Note the seashell embedded in the clay.

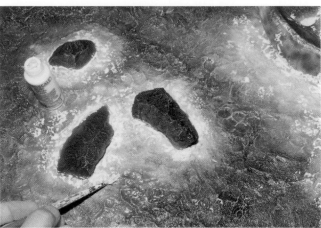

This Horizon *Elasmosaurus* has been cut in half and glued firmly to the base board. The tail was removed and similarly mounted. DIY interior fine-surface Polyfilla, applied with a broad spatula to give the impression of waves, formed the seascape.

Once the sea has been painted, any gaps between the model, rocks, and sculpted surface are filled with Kristal Klear. When the whole model is fully dry, spray it with a gloss lacquer.

Female plesiosaurs may have come ashore to lay eggs, like modern day turtles, and this could be an another way to display your model. Another would be to incorporate marine reptiles in a seascape created using traditional methods of sculpted plaster, suitably painted and gloss varnished to simulate water. This will work extremely well because you have complete control over how waves and ripples will look, especially important when integrating models and rocks into the diorama.

Plaster of paris is a good medium for modeling seascapes, as is white DasPronto or even fine-surface Polyfilla. These will cover large areas at a relatively low cost. You can use epoxy fillers, but they can prove expensive, unless the scene is a very small one.

DasPronto's or Polyfilla's slow drying time can prove advantageous, especially if the clay is watered down slightly. Broad-blade putty knives or large spatulas are ideal for sculpting water and oceans. Try to study the sea whenever possible, taking notes. Better yet, use color photographs for vital reference when modeling.

For the seascape illustrated, I chose Horizon's 1/30 scale vinyl *Elasmosaurus*. The body was sectioned with a razor saw and firmly secured to a wood-framed base board with pins and super glue. No real need for a precise match; the clay sea will hide any large gaps. Include a few rocks for added effect, then apply the clay and sculpt to create your ocean surface.

Water colors, which are easily mixed, seem to work best for painting seascapes. Recommended basic colors for tropical waters are various shades of blue, green, or turquoise. White and pale blue tones look effective around rocks, and using these colors for dry-brushing the peaks and troughs of the sculpted surface will increase realism. On my model, the rocks and *Elasmosaurus* were painted in situ before the sea colors were applied. Airbrushing white spray around the base of the rocks and around the premounted model is recommended before running Kristal Klear around all the lower edges. Droplets of water falling off the *Elasmosaurus* can be simulated by blobs of Kristal Klear applied via a fine brush or toothpick. When dry, the whole lot can be given several sprayed coats of high gloss lacquer. Artist's fixing sprays are ideal for this purpose, but don't breathe in the fumes!

As a final touch, perch a pterosaur on one of the rocks. We're going to look at these next.

FLYING DRAGONS

While dinosaurs reigned over the Earth and marine reptiles ruled the waves, Mesozoic skies were dominated by the pterosaurs. Ranging in size from delicate creatures the size of a pigeon to awesome monsters whose wingspans rivaled most World War II fighter airplanes, these flying reptiles make fascinating model subjects. *Pteranodon ingens* remains the most popular and has been kitted several times, but only the rare 1/35 scale Tamiya version can be seriously considered; the Airfix and Aurora efforts are crude and inaccurate. In recent years, the ever-prolific Kaiyodo has produced a high-standard trio of resin pterosaurs. This includes the giant *Quetzalcoatlus*.

You can greatly improve the appearance of pterosaur kits by replacing thickly molded wings with thin membrous versions of liquid latex rubber. The methods employed to achieve this are somewhat different from those previously described and a little more difficult to

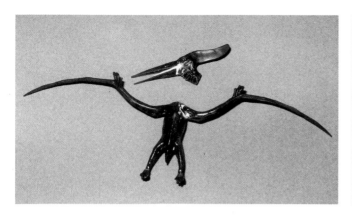

Tamiya's *Pteranodon* has had its beak cut apart and the lower half reglued as shown. Filler serves for the tongue and resulting neck gap. The really tricky part is cutting away the molded wing areas.

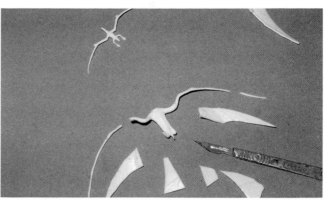

Removing wings from resin pterosaurs is an even more delicate operation. Score along the edges gently. Even with care, it's still possible to snap the fragile arms and fingers. See—I did! Not to worry. Just super glue them back together later.

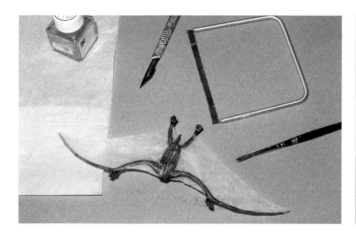

Remember Renwal's aeroskin? Well, this is Rimell's pteroskin! Model airplane tissue is cut to shape and glued to body, legs, arms, and wing fingers with liquid poly cement. Trim off excess material with a Flexi-File.

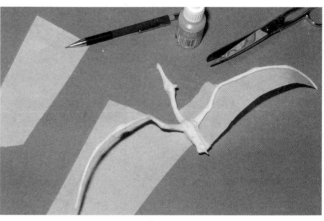

For sticking tissue to resin, super glue is the preferred adhesive. Now spray the tissue wings with water. When they are dry, apply a few coats of cellulose dope on the tissue areas only. Avoid doping plastic, resin, or vinyl material.

accomplish. Don't think that writers of modeling books never make mistakes or that their recommended techniques are foolproof. I tried three times to create realistic latex wings without success before I finally hit upon a method that worked to my satisfaction.

The first step is to cut off the molded wings, a procedure not recommended for the fainthearted. On plastic kits like Tamiya's *Pteranodon,* the wings are removed by careful and gradual scoring along the body sides, legs, upper arms, and elongated fourth wing finger. Be patient. Don't be tempted to break off the wing sections until the cuts are almost through the plastic. Clean up all the cut edges with file and sandpaper; if any gaps appear along the body side, now's the time to fill them. Resin models are treated in exactly the same way, but the material is very brittle and you can count yourself lucky if you manage to remove the molded

wings without snapping an arm or a leg. But, as they say, you can't make an omelette without breaking a few eggs.

PTEROSKIN

Cut out the wing membrane from white or pale pink flying–model airplane tissue. Use scissors to cut to shape and use the kit parts as a template or refer to scientific drawings. For plastic kits, use polystyrene tube or liquid cement, or both, to attach the tissue panels and use super glue for resin models. This requires a deft touch, and the glue should be applied sparingly at intervals to anchor the tissue. Run glue along all edges, and when it is dry, trim and sand the leading edge and body joints.

You will now need to tauten the tissue by airbrushing or spraying with water. After drying, brush on

Yes, it's latex time again! Paint in the veins with matte enamels before adding liquid latex to both surfaces of the tissue. Apply it liberally around the arms and legs. When it's dry, airbrush the tissue-covered, latex-coated wings in your chosen color scheme. Light coats *only*—you don't want to lose the translucent effect the pteroskin gives you!

a coat or two of model airplane cellulose shrinking dope to seal it. You should now have a fairly stiff, glossy wing surface on which you can paint blood vessels with enamel paint. Once you've done that, apply two coats of latex rubber to the lower surface area of the tissue and four or more to the upper surfaces.

Leave to dry before completing the model prior to final painting.

I've tried the technique on large and small pterosaurs, and it works equally well, even on the tiny *Nyctosaurus* models found in Tamiya's *Parasaurolophus* diorama kit. If carefully airbrushed, the translucent wings can look extremely realistic.

Research shows that many, if not all, pterosaurs were covered in fur. I've not found a really effective way of reproducing this feature on small scale models, but for larger ones, you could add strips of fake fur fixed with super glue. On 1/35 scale pterosaurs, simple drybrushing may suffice.

SOURCES

DINOSAUR MANUFACTURERS, SCULPTORS, AND AGENTS

Alternative Images, 1237 Fort Hunter Rd., Schenectady, NY 12303. 518-355-7958.

CM Studio, 600 N. Adams St., Gillespie, IL 62033. 217-839-2593.

The Dinosaur Studio, 116 Bowdoin St., Medford, MA 02155. 508-897-3636.

Dragon Attack! 1220 Amethyst St., Mentone, CA 92359. 909-794-4755.

Dragon Inc., 15 Sandalwood Dr., Smithtown, NY 11787. 516-724-6583.

Glencoe Models, P. O. Box 846, Northboro, MA 01532. 508-869-6877.

Hell Creek Creations, 1208 Nashua La., Hanover Park, IL 60103. 708-289-7018.

Heroes from Another Planet, 861 Sutter St., 300 San Francisco, CA 94109. 415-673-1838.

Horizon Hobbies and Toys, 912 E. Third St., Ste. 101, Los Angeles, CA 90013.

Invicta, from Advancing Play, 1789 Maryland Ave., Niagara Falls, NY 14305. 800-565-6386.

Kaiyodo, available from Monstrosities, P. O. Box 1024, North Baldwin, NY 11510. 516-378-1338.

Lindberg, Craft House, 328 N. Westwood Ave., Toledo, OH 43607.

Link & Pin Hobbies, Triceratops Hills Ranch, 7868 S. Magnolia Way, Englewood, CO 80112. 303-741-4712.

Lunar Models, P. O. Box 733, Cleburne, TX 76033. 817-556-0296.

Menagerie Productions, 535 Alabama St., San Francisco, CA 94110. 415-861-2570.

Monsters in Motion, 330 E. Orangethorpe, Unit H, Placentia, CA 92670. 714-577-8863.

Revell, 8601 Waukegan Rd., Morton Grove, IL 60053-2295. 708-866-3500.

Saurian Studios, 83 Brook Rd., Weston, MA 02193. 617-894-5160.

Tamiya America, 2 Orion, Aliso Viejo, CA 92656-4200. 800-826-4922.

Tsukuda, available from International Hobby Supply, 8839 Shirley Ave., Northridge, CA 91324. 818-886-3113.

Wiccart, 2109, 33 King St., Weston, ON M9N, Canada. 416-243-5017.

MATERIALS

Celluclay: Activa Products, P. O. Box 472, Westford, MA 75760.

Glass eyes: Eyedentity Products, Woodview, Aberhafesp, Nr. Newton, Powys, SY16 3HC, Wales.

Milliput: VLS Mail Order, 811 Lone Star Drive, Lone Star Industrial Park, O'Fallon, MO 63366. 314-281-5700.

Photoetched foliage: Scale Link Ltd., Rear of Talbot Hotel, Blandford Rd., Iwerne Minster, Dorset, DT11 8QN, England. 44-747-811817.

Super Sculpey from Polyform, 1901 Estes Ave., Elk Grove Village, IL 60007.

BIBLIOGRAPHY

General Dinosaur References

Augusta, Josef. *Prehistoric Sea Monsters* (Paul Hamlyn, London, 1964).

Augusta, Josef. *The Age of Monsters* (Paul Hamlyn, London, 1966).

Benton, Michael J. *The Reign of the Reptiles* (Kingfisher Books, London, 1990).

Carpenter, K., Hirsch, K.F., and Horner, J. (editors). *Dinosaur Eggs and Babies* (Cambridge University Press, New York, 1994).

Czerkas, Sylvia, J., and Olson, Everett, C. (editors). *Dinosaurs Past and Present,* Volumes I and II (Natural History Museum of Los Angeles County in association with University of Washington Press, Seattle and London, 1987).

Czerkas, Sylvia, J., and Czerkas, Stephen A. *Dinosaurs: A Global View* (Mallard Press, New York, 1991).

Dixon, Dougal, Cox, B., Savage, R. J. G., and Gardiner, B. (editors). *The MacMillan Illustrated Encyclopedia of Dinosaurs and Prehistoric Animals: A Visual Who's Who of Prehistoric Life* (MacMillan Publishing Company, New York, 1988).

Gardom, Tim. *The Natural History Museum Book of Dinosaurs* (Virgin Books, London, 1993).

Gould, Stephen, J. (general editor). *The Book of Life: An Illustrated History of the Evolution of Life on Earth* (W. W. Norton and Company, New York, 1993).

Knight, Charles, R. *Animal Drawing: Anatomy and Action for Artists* (1947, Dover Publications, Inc., New York, 1959).

Lambert, David. *The Ultimate Dinosaur Book* (Dorling Kindersley, London/New York/Stuttgart, 1993).

Lindsay, William. *Barosaurus/Corythosaurus/Triceratops/ Tyrannosaurus* (Natural History Museum series of four titles, Dorling Kindersley, London, 1992–1993.)

Norman, David. *Dinosaur!* (Prentice Hall, New York, 1991).

Norman, David. *The Illustrated Encyclopedia of Dinosaurs* (Crescent Books, New York, 1985).

Norman, David. *Prehistoric Life* (Boxtree, London, 1994).

Parker, Steve. *The Rise of the Dinosaurs* (Dragon's World, Surrey, 1994).

Parker, Steve. *The Triumph of the Dinosaurs* (Dragon's World, Surrey, 1994).

Paul, Gregory, S. *Predatory Dinosaurs of the World: A Complete Illustrated Guide* (Simon and Schuster, New York, 1988).

Preiss, B., and Silverberg, R. (editors). *The Ultimate Dinosaur* (Bantam Books, New York, 1992).

Psihoyos, Louis. *Hunting Dinosaurs* (Cassell, London, 1994).

Russell, D. A. *An Odyssey in Time: The Dinosaurs of North America* (University of Toronto Press, National Museum of Natural Sciences, 1989).

Sattler, Helen Roney. *The New Illustrated Dinosaur Dictionary* (Lothrop, Lee and Shepard Books, New York, 1990).

Shay, Dan, and Duncan, Jody. *The Making of Jurassic Park* (Ballantine Trade, 1993).

Sibbick, John, and Hawcock, David. *Tyrannosaurus Rex: The Tyrant King,* (Tango Books, London, 1995).

Spinar, Zdenek. *Life Before Man,* illustrated by Zdenek Burian (Thames and Hudson Ltd., London, 1995).

Stout, William. *The Dinosaurs: A Fantastic View of a Lost Era* (Mallard Press, New York, 1981).

The Visual Dictionary of Dinosaurs (Dorling Kindersley, London, 1993).

Wallace, Joseph. *The American Museum of Natural History's Book of Dinosaurs and Other Ancient Creatures* (Michael Friedman Publishing Group, New York, 1994).

Weishampel, D. B., Dodson, P., and Osmolska, H. (editors). *The Dinosauria* (University of California Press, 1990).

Wellnhoffer, Peter. *The Illustrated Encyclopedia of Pterosaurs: An Illustrated History of the Flying Reptiles of the Mesozoic Era* (Crescent Books, New York, 1991).

References for Modeling

Araki, Kazunari. *Fifty Dinosaurs* (Dainipponkaiga Co. Ltd., 1993).

Araki, Kazunari. *The Dinosaur Sculptures* (Dainipponkaiga, 1987).

Boyer, Paul. *Painting and Finishing Scale Models* (Kalmbach Books, Wisconsin, 1993).

Goldman, Larry. *How to Create Water and Ice and Other Good "Stuff"* (Hide and Beak Taxidermy and Supply Co., Minnesota, 1983).

Kesler, Lynn, and Winar, Don. *How To Paint Realistic Military Figures* (Kalmbach Books, Wisconsin, 1993).

Lanteri, Edouard. *Modeling and Sculpting Animals* (1911, Dover Publications, Inc., New York, 1985).

Morales, Bob, and Debus, Allen and Diane. *Dinosaur Sculpting* (Hell Creek Creations, Illinois, 1995).

Paine, Shepherd. *How to Build Dioramas* (Kalmbach Books, Wisconsin, 1980).

Tajima, Teruhisa. *Dinosaur Photographs* (Dinopix) (Kadokawashoten, Japan, 1994).

Williamson, Bob (general editor). *The Breakthrough Habitat and Exhibit Manual* (Breakthrough Publications, Loganville, 1986).

Dinosaur Journals and Societies

Archosaurian Archive. Bi-monthly. Wiccart, PH3, 33 King St., Weston, ON M9N 3R7, Canada.

The Dinosaur Report. The Quarterly Journal of The Dinosaur Society Inc., 200 Carleton Ave., East Islip, NY 11730.

The Dinosaur Society UK Quarterly. The Journal of The Dinosaur Society UK, P. O. Box 329, Canterbury, Kent, CT4 5GB, U.K.

Model Dinosaur. Quarterly newsletter (editor, Ray Rimell). 10 Long View, Berkhamsted, Herts, HP4 1BY, U.K.

Prehistoric Times. Bi-monthly (editor, Mike Fredericks). 145 Bayline Circle, Folsom, CA 95630.